Against Capitalism

"The hardest trick for a historian to pull off, especially when engaged in a work aimed at a broad readership, is to tell an interesting story without sacrificing analysis and explanation. In his history of the rise of the European radical Left in the half-century following the foundation of the International Working Men's Association in 1871, William A. Pelz has performed this feat admirably. Although this revolutionary Left failed in its goal of destroying capitalism as a basis of political power and instituting a classless society, it played a major and positive role in creating the world we know. Pelz explains this paradox, while maintaining a well-paced narrative of the individual men and women, sometimes heroic and sometimes less so, who built and staffed this movement."

Steven McGiffen, Editor of Spectre Magazine *(France);*
Visiting Professor of International Relations, American Graduate School
of International Relations and Diplomacy, Paris

"Criticisms of a world governed by the marketplace rather than by people have become all the more timely with the acknowledged global environmental crisis and the ever-tighter control of money over the political processes in capitalist societies. Students interested in a historical perspective on these questions will find William A. Pelz's *Against Capitalism* a coherent, concise, and accurate description of the emergence of the European Left and its enduring significance. This book is a real gem!"

Mark Lause, Professor of History, University of Cincinnati

"This is a very useful introduction to the adolescent years of socialism in Europe. It clearly demonstrates how very differently socialists looked for answers to very diverse national problems and how difficult it was to find international unity. More important, the book shows the significance of these different socialist ideals and movements for the development and the emancipation of the individual. This is why, at the beginning of this new century, social ideals continue to attract great interest in Europe and elsewhere in the world."

Ronald van Raak, Member of Dutch Parliament, Socialist Party of the Netherlands

Against Capitalism

Studies in Modern European History

Frank J. Coppa
General Editor

Vol. 52

PETER LANG
New York • Washington, D.C./Baltimore • Bern
Frankfurt am Main • Berlin • Brussels • Vienna • Oxford

William A. Pelz

Against Capitalism

The European Left
on the March

PETER LANG
New York • Washington, D.C./Baltimore • Bern
Frankfurt am Main • Berlin • Brussels • Vienna • Oxford

Library of Congress Cataloging-in-Publication Data

Pelz, William A.
Against capitalism: the European left on the march / William A. Pelz.
p. cm. — (Studies in modern European history; v. 52)
Includes bibliographical references and index.
1. Socialism—Europe—History. 2. Radicalism—Europe—History.
3. Revolutions—Europe—History. 4. Europe—History—1871–1918. I. Title.
HX238.P45   335.094—dc22   2007016395
ISBN 978-0-8204-6776-4
ISSN 0893-6897

Bibliographic information published by **Die Deutsche Bibliothek.**
Die Deutsche Bibliothek lists this publication in the "Deutsche
Nationalbibliografie"; detailed bibliographic data is available
on the Internet at http://dnb.ddb.de/.

The paper in this book meets the guidelines for permanence and durability
of the Committee on Production Guidelines for Book Longevity
of the Council of Library Resources.

© 2007 Peter Lang Publishing, Inc., New York
29 Broadway, 18th floor, New York, NY 10006
www.peterlang.com

Printed in Germany

This modest work is dedicated to all those ordinary women and men, whose names are now lost to history, who struggled for a more just, equal world. Their dreams have not been realized—but—neither have their struggles been in vain.

Contents

Acknowledgments...xi

Introduction...1

1. European Radicalism in the 1870s....................................5
   International Working Men's Association............................5
   Impact of the IWMA...9
   Franco-Prussian War and the Paris Commune....................10
   The Commune in Power...12
   Fall of the Paris Commune...14
   Significance of the Commune...15

2. Birth and Development of Left Radicalism after 1871..............17
   Rise of the Trade Unions...17
   Creation of Socialist Political Parties................................23
   Founding of the Second International...............................29
   The Socialist International and May Day............................30
   Women Workers and Socialism.......................................34
   Anarchism..36
   Syndicalism..39
   Failure of Repression..41
   Anti-Socialist Law in Germany, 1878–1890.......................42

3. Splits within the European Left Before World War I..............45
   Revisionist Controversy in Germany................................46
   The Millerand Affair in France..50
   The Split in Russian Socialism.......................................52
   Anarchist Alienation from Socialism................................54
   Syndicalism's Challenge to Socialism...............................56
   European Radicalism: The View from Below.......................59
   The European Left at the End of the 19th Century.................63

4. The Left Confronts Militarism, Colonialism and Rebellion......65
Militarism and the Threat of War..66
Encountering the Problem of Colonialism............................70
The Case of the Boer War..73
The Socialist International and Colonialism..........................76
Russia's Revolutionary Dress Rehearsal of 1905....................77
Birth of the Soviets...80
The Left and the Council Movement....................................82
Mass Strike..83
Road to War...85
European Radicals and the Impending War...........................88

5. From War to Revolution, Europe 1914–1917..........................91
World War's Impact on Europe..94
Women and the War...95
Casualties during the War..96
Inception of Antiwar Activism...97
Zimmerwald..99
Divisions within Radical Organizations..............................101
March Revolution in Russia...104
All Power to the Soviets...106
Bolsheviks Come to Power..108

6. Revolutionary Europe, 1917–1921.................................111
The Kaiser Goes, the Generals Remain...............................112
Aborted Revolution in Germany.......................................114
Suppression of the Revolutionary Left...............................116
Collapse of the Hapsburg Monarchy.................................119
Austro-Marxism and Revolutionary Vienna........................119
Soviet Republic in Hungary...121
Collapse of the Soviet Government in Hungary....................123
Anti-Semitism and Revolutionary Movements.....................124
The First World War's Impact on Italy................................125
The Biennio Rosso in Northern Italy..................................126

Revolutionary Dissent in France........................128
Suppression of the Mutiny...............................129
Urban Unrest...130
The Easter Rebellion in Ireland.........................131
Rebellious Britain, 1918–1919...........................133
Ebbing of the Revolutionary Tide........................134

Conclusion: The Significance of Revolutionary Left in Europe...135
Reasons for Revolutionary Failures......................135
Legacy of the European Revolutionary Left...............141

Further Reading.......................................147
European Radicalism in 1871.............................148
Birth and Development of European Left Radicalism.......149
Splits within the European Left, 1898–1905..............151
Left Confronts Militarism, Colonialism and Rebellion....152
First World War and the Revolutionary Crisis, 1914–1921....153
Revolutionary Europe, 1917–1921.........................154

Index..157

Acknowledgments

A vast number of people have directly or indirectly contributed to the ideas and arguments contained in this book. Among those so implicated (in no particular order) are: Theo Bergmann, Steven McGiffen, Jean Pierre Page, Bruno Drwnski, Narihiko Ito, Ottokar Luban, Mario Kessler, Sobhanlal Datta Gupta, Morris Slavin, Alexandre Pantsov, Eric Schuster, Jeff Olson, Wesley Aten, DanParry, Mark Lause, Ronald Van Raak, and Jie-Hyun Lim. I ask forgiveness in advance to anyone who I may have omitted.

The strengths of this work are almost certainly theirs, the weaknesses mine. Most of all, I owe a huge debt to John Metz for his comments and suggestions as well as preparing the final manuscript for publication.

Introduction

Terms used to describe different political viewpoints like *left* and *right* may appear confusing. They *are* perplexing, in part, because so many people have used them to mean very different things. Taken from the physical positions where various groups sat in the National Assembly during the French Revolution, "right" means those committed to tradition while "left" means those who want change. Thus, someone who is "right-wing" is more committed to the status quo while someone who is more "left-wing" is more devoted to change. These terms have acquired other meanings as well. The "right" is generally opposed to equality and freedom. Thus, the monarchies mentioned in this book would be considered "right-wing" while the radicals who fought for free elections and social equality would be considered "left-wing." These are not the only terms which are often used in an imprecise or confusing way.

Today, the word *revolutionary* is frequently used to describe bath soaps or vegetable chopping machines while *socialism* is popularly equated with a failed dictatorship in Russia. Yet in Europe of little more than a century ago, there existed tremendously popular movements of common people who considered themselves both revolutionary and socialist. To these individuals, there was no contradiction between democracy and socialism. In fact, they considered socialism as a necessary part of democracy.

The members of these left-wing movements felt that only revolutionary transformations of their societies could create a world of justice and equality. To understand their politics, we must use our imagination to put ourselves in their shoes. These radicals were born, lived, and died in a world that was a much different place than ours is today. In nineteenth-century Europe, the vast majority of adults could not vote. In most nations, not even a majority of men could vote while in countries like Czarist Russia there were no elections at all. Of course, those who suggested that women should be granted suffrage were thought little better than mad by upper class society.

The prevailing theory of economy was based on the free market or capitalist view that no restrictions should burden business. The great industrialists and merchants, often referred to as the grand bourgeoisie—as opposed to small business or the petty bourgeoisie—considered they were building a world of freedom. Production in this period was based on free labor. That is by workers who were paid wages for the labor they performed. In turn, products saturated the free market, and the profits were reaped by those who owned the means of production—factories, machinery, and land. The free workers, frequently called proletarians, in the view of the bourgeoisie, should work hard and save money in order to get ahead. Somehow, the mass of laborers did not tend to share these convictions. This was very different from previous centuries when most of Europe's people were serfs who were bound to the land and forced to pay tribute—often two-thirds of all they produced—to their lord.

Throughout nineteenth-century Europe wave after wave of peasants were dispossessed of land—albeit at disparate rapidity in different countries—and forced to look for work in the cities. In addition, the increased productivity of agriculture helped support an important population increase. Crowding into the slums of the ever-expanding urban areas, these former peasants started new lives as workers. They found wages low, hours long, and extended periods of unemployment inevitable. As brutal as farm labor had been, they had responded to the rhythms of nature. Now, they were slaves to the clock. The proud, if poor, European peasant was transformed into the angry worker who was now told when to eat, when he could talk, when he could relieve himself. The thought of being awoken by a machine (the alarm clock) may not be alien today, but it was foreign to these new proletarians.

Likewise, the European artisan—the shoemaker, the weaver, the tailor—found that the new world of workshops and factories was a bitter place. As the quality of their product could no longer compete with the quantity of cheap goods produced by machines, they too were pushed into the factory. Once protected by their skill and possessing the tools of production, they saw themselves turned from craftsmen into servants of machines.

For most of the nineteenth century, European governments did not provide social programs that would improve the average worker's quality of life. There existed little, if any, public education throughout most of the continent. There were no social security or workers' compensation laws. Few minimum wage laws existed, whereas trade unions spent much of the 1800s outlawed and hounded by even the most liberal European governments. Health care, if available at all, was primitive at best: many popular over-the-counter medicines were crude concoctions of alcohol, sugar, and opium. In England, birth place of the industrial revolution, the life expectancy of workers in the 1840s was less than half that of businessmen.

Treated little better than cattle by many employers, workers scraped out an existence which offered little joy or hope of rapid improvement. Little wonder that excessive alcohol consumption and sexual license became the norm in many factory towns. Many workers saw drink as one of their few pleasures in life, while more than a few mothers with hungry children found prostitution their only source of income. In nineteenth-century England, for example, some estimates suggest that as many as one woman out of five was a full-time prostitute for at least some portion of her life.

One twenty-four year old German businessman, shocked at the state of England's workers, wrote, in 1844, of the destruction of the family by capitalist society: "In a comfortless, filthy house, hardly good enough for mere night shelter, ill-furnished, often neither rainproof nor warm, a foul atmosphere filling rooms overcrowded with human beings, no domestic comfort is possible. The husband works the whole day through, perhaps the wife also and the elder children, all in different places; they meet night and morning only, all under perpetual temptation to drink; what family life is possible under such conditions?" The author of these observations—in his *The Condition of the Working Class in England*—was Frederick Engels (1820–1895) who would four years later coauthor the *Communist Manifesto* with Karl Marx (1818–1883).

Nor was this sense of outrage unique to Engels. Many Europeans regarded the world created by industrial capitalism as one where the living envied the dead. They believed that Christian and traditional moral values were being destroyed along with countless human lives. In response, large numbers of workers increasingly found politics more intoxicating than gin and fought to develop trade unions and labor-based political parties.

These enraged workers were to become radicals who sought to build a new world based on equality instead of inequality: they placed an emphasis on democracy rather than rule by an elite and valued cooperation over competition. Although their dream was never realized, in the process of fighting for it, they won numerous reforms which have made the world a different place today. For example, the now mainly accepted concept of universal, free education was considered subversive and communist in the nineteenth century. Whether attracted or repulsed by the ideals of the revolutionary left, anyone who seeks to comprehend European history must understand them.

Because the most pivotal centers of radical thought and action was in the urban area, this text will concentrate primarily on cities and their inhabitants. Thus, the actions of the peasantry will largely be outside the scope of this work. Another question might be asked about the period chosen since it does not correspond to normal periodization. In other words, why 1871 to 1921 not 1848 to 1914 or 1815 to 1914? This apparently unusual time period was selected because it starts with the period of the rise and growth of socialism and radicals in the 1870s. It continues through the critical period of war and revolution in the early twentieth century ending with the defeat of the more radical revolutionary movements and the beginning of the rise of fascism. Since the whole question of fascism and the left's response is a large and complex one—easily requiring another book—this volume ends in 1921.

1. European Radicalism in the 1870s

For European radicals, the year 1871 was, as Charles Dickens wrote in another context, "the best of times and the worst of times." The best of times in that the creation of the short-lived Paris Commune gave revolutionaries of myriad ideologies an example of the new democratic society they sought to build. Further, the ever increasing industrialization of Europe created legions of new workers whose condition made them sympathetic to the platform of the left. As the number and self-confidence of workers grew so did the potential for mass radical movements. For example, in 1875 the German Social Democratic Party was formed. It would, eventually, become the largest mass membership left-wing party in Europe with a membership of over a million by 1914.

Still, it was the worst of times in that the revolutionary left—those who thought society needed to be completely transformed—was in headlong retreat during most of the 1870s. The destruction of the Paris Commune in 1871 and the resulting repression by the French Government resulted in the death or exile of tens of thousands of radicals while those who remained at liberty were fearful and uncertain as the new conservative government hunted them down. Ideological disputes tore the once promising International Working Men's Association, the so-called First International, into warring factions and finally led to its dissolution. Governments across the continent wielded repression against all brands of labor radicalism, regarding most leftists as little better than bomb throwing lunatics.

International Working Men's Association

To understand the crucial decade of the 1870s, an examination of the revolutionary left's advances and retreats is warranted. The much misunderstood International Working Men's Association (IWMA) is a fitting starting point for such an analysis. Feared by reactionaries as the general staff of a massive international conspiracy, the IWMA was the first notable attempt to develop a worldwide organization of workers. Although short lived and far less influential than conservatives frequently feared, the International nevertheless promoted the revolutionary notion of transcontinental labor solidarity.

On September 28, 1864, representatives of British and French workers met in London's St. Martin's Hall to establish an association which would help coordinate labor activities. The International Working Men's Association was not initiated to promote revolution or socialism but to act as a sort of worker's United Nations. According to the General Rules of the IWMA, its purpose was "to afford a central medium of communication and cooperation between Working Men's Societies existing in different countries." Membership was open to all workers' organizations regardless of ideology although most were inclined towards socialism. Unlike the later Socialist International or Second International, the IWMA was not a federation of national parties. Rather, it consisted of individual members who joined local sections in their country. Still, it had significant backing from a number of, particularly British, trade unions.

Despite the "International" goals of the IWMA, it was always a European, in fact mainly a Western European, organization. Even in Europe, the International Working Men's Association was not the primary reason that radical movements did, or did not, develop in any individual country. Whether the IWMA was strongly supported in any nation appears to have had little impact on the level of radical struggle.

Still, the bourgeois or conservative press quickly came to see the hand of the International behind every display of public unrest and strike action. The London *Times*, for instance, estimated the IWMA membership at 2,500,000 while a German official claimed to have proof that more than 5,000,000 was secretly on deposit in the Association's London bank account. Such frequent and hysterical reactions greatly exaggerated the International's actual deeds, and in turn, offered the public an inaccurate image of the organization. Thus, those among the right-wing, conservative members of European society imagined a massive conspiracy drawing upon an enormous war chest, while radical workers believed that they had a powerful benefactor.

Both the enemies and the supporters of the International were wrong. Far from being well funded, the IWMA started with a yearly income of thirty-three pounds sterling and financial matters never really improved. In fact, Frederick Engels once joked that great sum of money that the International had amassed was largely in debts. Furthermore, all the evidence suggests that European radicals acted independently of the International and it received the blame (or credit) after the fact. Why then did such a modest organization gain such a gigantic reputation?

One answer can be found in the organization's most famous member. Although he was not the initial organizer of the International Working Men's Association, Karl Marx quickly became its most prominent leader, working from his London exile. Marx, and later Engels, became almost synonymous with the International. Not only did Marx fashion the public statements from the IWMA's General Council in London in the manner of a revolutionary challenge to capitalism, but also his work performed outside of the organization was identified with it. Thus in 1867, the completion of the massive first volume of *Das Kapital* served to enhance the reputation of both its author and the organization with which he was associated. This book was to contribute a theoretical framework for the European left, although numerous radicals who considered themselves Marxists never truly understood it—if they read it at all. Even Marx's own mother is reported to have scolded her son with the lament, "If only you had made capital instead of written it."

On a more practical level, the International did involve itself in any number of prudent projects. The IWMA helped with strike support by collecting money and preventing strike breakers from crossing national borders. It promoted the self-organization of the working class and undoubtedly contributed to the increase of trade unions in the 1860s. Although their puny treasury and modest active membership made the IWMA powerless to initiate actions, when radicals launched political endeavors, they often did so in the name of the International. That is, many more people *felt* they were part of the International than ever actually paid dues.

After the defeat of France by Prussia in the Franco-Prussian War, the rebellious French workers instigated a successful coup in Paris and declared the city a commune on March 28, 1871. They did so against the advice of Marx who had warned the IWMA's Paris section it would be folly to attempt a revolution under the current circumstance of Prussian military presence and general collapse following the French defeat. He feared that Paris would quickly be isolated from the rest of France while the victorious Prussians would directly or indirectly have the military might to crush the rebellion. Yet once the Commune was established with the help of the Paris IWMA members, the International was obliged to defend it. Two days after the fall of the Commune, on May 30, 1871, Marx delivered an address to the General Council of the IWMA which was later published as *The Civil War in France.* Thereafter, the Paris Commune was attributed to an organization which had neither enough power to cause it nor enough support to prevent it.

In the years following the fall of the Paris Commune, the revolutionary movement throughout most of Europe underwent a sharp decline. Likewise, the International Working Men's Association experienced a similar weakening. By supporting the Commune, the IWMA lost the support of moderate English trade unionists, while those members who remained loyal to the organization faced increased police repression—arrests, suppression of their newspapers, exile. With the IWMA in such a weakened condition, Marx and other socialist members of the organization were unable to confront the growing challenge of anarchists within the International. Anarchists represented a very different radical current from that associated with Marx. They had lost all patience with slow educational activity or attempts to work for reforms within existing institutions. Anarchists did not even believe there should be a government or state after the revolution. The members of this tendency believed in direct action and even assassination to achieve their goal of a stateless society. The anarchists considered themselves "libertarians" who fought against Marx and his "dictatorship" in the International. In actuality, Marx was far from being a dictator. He was, after all, supported by moderate trade unionists who were more sympathetic to his vision of socialism than to the specter of exploding anarchist bombs.

As the battles between the socialist revolutionaries and their anarchists critics became sharper, the existence of the IWMA became increasingly pointless. Never a strong, unified organization, the International was split by disputes which had a strong national basis. The socialists drew their support from industrialized northern European areas, such as Germany, while the anarchists drew members from the southern countries like Spain and Italy. To end an impossible situation, Marx and Engels won a majority in 1872 for their motion transferring the General Council to the United States. There, the IWMA quickly died, being formally dissolved in Philadelphia in July, 1876.

Impact of the IWMA

The International Working Men's Association had lasted little more than a decade. If one were to judge an organization by longevity, the IWMA is hardly worth more than a footnote in a history book. Yet, its shadow was always larger than its substance. While the IWMA failed to establish an ongoing working class organization, much less a successful general staff of revolution, it did accomplish much of great importance. Most of all, the organization popularized certain concepts which were to become central to the growth of the revolutionary left. Among these were 1) the idea of working class self-emancipation, 2) the opinion that capitalism would not last forever and was not the "end of history," 3) the belief that international solidarity among exploited and oppressed people could overcome nationalistic passions, 4) the conviction that revolution was not a dream but would one day be a reality.

But, the IWMA was more than an organization which ignored the pressing matters of the day in favor of lofty theoretical pronouncements. It welcomed reforms which improved the condition of workers such as the Great Britain's *Ten Hours Act of 1847*—which limited the hours a worker could be forced to labor—and gradualist experiments like the cooperative movement which sought to establish nonprofit companies which would benefit both worker and consumers. Even in the field of foreign policy, far from abstaining from involvement, the First International took principled and often courageous platforms. The case of the Civil War in the United States is one such example.

Although British textile workers suffered bitterly because of the cotton shortage caused by the North's blockade of the Confederacy, the IWMA expressed its solidarity with Abraham Lincoln and helped rally workers to support the struggle against African-American slavery. Formed shortly before the 1864 Presidential election, one of the International's first acts was to send an address of congratulations, written by Marx, to Lincoln, that "single-minded son of the working class." Since textiles were vital to the British economy, a section of the middle class and a large portion of the upper class were demanding armed intervention to break the Northern States' blockade. The IWMA was instrumental in organizing against this possibility and, thus, helped prevent a British military adventure which might have been disastrous for Lincoln, the Northern States, and the struggle to abolish slavery. The First International would become an important part of the revolutionary mythology which would inspire generations of European militants—as did the Paris Commune.

Franco-Prussian War and the Paris Commune

Much like the International, the Paris Commune is a historical event shrouded in historical fictions. While it is fact that the common people of Paris ruled themselves in the spring of 1871, it is fiction that the uprising was part of some sort of international conspiracy or that a revolutionary plan existed. The reality is fascinating enough, even without the legends.

Paris was, in many ways, the most politically radical city of Europe. Not only had the key events of the French Revolution of 1789 been played out on the Parisian streets, but the revolutions of 1830 and 1848 had also taken place there. In his dictatorship, Louis Bonaparte (1808–1873), self-named Napoleon III, had suppressed revolutionary sentiments from his coup d'état in 1851 until the collapse of his "Second Empire" during the Franco-Prussian War of 1870–1871. Tricked into war by the Prussian leader Otto von Bismarck (1815–1898), Bonaparte was soon captured and his army crushed.

After the collapse of the Second Empire and Bonaparte's capture, France was once again declared a republic and a new legislative Assembly was elected to negotiate with Bismarck. This new legislature was staunchly reactionary—nearly two-thirds of those elected were monarchists. Yet, the Assembly was unable to restore a king to the throne mainly because its members were divided into two factions which supported competing wings of the royal family. Faced with Bismarck's harsh terms, the royalist Assembly felt it had no other choice but to give in. The Assembly relinquished part of eastern France, Alsace-Lorraine, to the newly created German Empire. In addition, a large reparation was to be paid to Germany, and Paris was to be occupied by the victorious Prussian Army.

Given the tremendous sacrifice given during and frightful suffering caused by the war, it is not surprising that Paris reacted with outraged fury to announcement of the surrender terms. As the feeling of betrayal became more widespread, revolutionary feeling grew among the lower classes while many of the upper class fled the metropolis. Members of the National Guard—an organization of commoners not unlike that in the U.S.—became openly defiant of their commanders, who were imposed by the national government. In order to protect themselves from what they saw as treachery, radicals seized arms and artillery. As the National Guard reorganized itself on a more democratic and representative basis under a new Central Committee, talk of armed resistance to the Prussians flourished. Concerned that the revolutionary attitudes of Paris might infect his troops and seeing no benefit from fighting prolonged street battles, Bismarck wisely avoided forcing such a confrontation. Instead, the Prussian army contented itself to occupy a small area of Paris for a mere two days before withdrawing to the northern and eastern forts. Bismarck made sure that no attempt was made to occupy the working class districts of the French capital.

With the speedy withdrawal of Prussian soldiers, the streets of Paris filled once more with noisy demonstrations. The reactionary Assembly threw fuel on the revolutionary fire by a series of decrees ordering the immediate payment of overdue rents and bills. Many Parisians, including numerous small businessmen, would have been ruined by obedience to this law. Further, the Assembly showed its fear of, if not contempt for, Paris by choosing to meet at Versailles, the palace of French kings. As relations between the new government and Paris grew ever tenser, more troops were sent into the capital to maintain order. As these soldiers grew more sympathetic to the plight of the Parisians, the Versailles government decided to remove them and all government offices from the radical city. Adolphe Thiers (1797–1877), leader of the government at Versailles, hoped he could buy time until a new army could be built to crush revolutionary Paris once and for all. Afterwards, Thiers would claim businessmen had warned that financial matters would not start up again "until all those wretches [in Paris] were finished off."

The Commune in Power

After the Assembly had abandoned Paris, the only authority left was the National Guard who reluctantly took up administration of the city. Declaring it had no mandate to be the government, the Central Committee of the National Guard decided to hold elections to create a representative government. On March 26, 1871, elections to what was called "The Commune of Paris" took place. Voting privileges were given to all adult males and over a quarter of a million votes were cast. Two days later on March 28 as the red flag flew over Paris, one of the most radical governments ever seen in Europe took office— radical in the sense of being more democratic and equalitarian than previous regimes.

The new leaders averaged thirty-eight years in age and often lacked political experience. Of the eight-one members elected to the Commune, approximately thirty-five were blue collar workers while about forty were professionals of one sort or another. Among these men were about forty people with background in the French labor movement and perhaps as many as nineteen members of the International Working Men's Association, although few of the latter were Marxists.

But the most unique characteristic of the Commune was neither the history nor the class backgrounds that its leaders brought to it. The Commune's structure was an experiment in democracy. Rather than electing members to the Commune who then would do what they thought best, the duties of the representatives were seen quite literally. That is, they were to undertake what those who elected them wanted done. Thus, Commune members had the duty to remain in constant contact with those who elected them. This aim was backed up by the institution of immediate recall of any Commune member whose constituents found his performance lacking. Even so, many members became entrenched in seemingly endless debates and the day-to-day business of government.

It was a government which genuinely sought to make life better for the working and middle classes. Although the continued existence of private property was not questioned per se, a number of radical reforms were instituted. In contrast to the harsh Versailles law that required immediate repayment, the Commune voted for a three-year delay in the reimbursement of rents and overdue bills. To eliminate unemployment and increase production, it was decided to allow trade unions and workers' cooperative to take over factories not in use. While previously one-third of Paris's children had received no formal education at all, the Commune made education a major priority. Not only was a basic education for all mandated by the Commune, it placed special emphasis on women's education. A special Commission composed entirely of women was given the task of overseeing female education while day care centers were opened near factories to help working women.

Of course, none of these or the countless other innovative plans drafted by the Commune ever had time to undergo extensive development. In fact, it is amazing that—given the conditions of isolation, shortages and Versailles harassment—anything at all was accomplished. Paris was isolated from the rest of France. Communes were attempted in a few other urban areas such as Marseille and Lyon but all were rapidly put down. Anti-Commune sentiment seized the peasantry, due largely to the efforts of the Versailles government and its allies in the Roman Catholic Church. The Church painted Paris in shades which were nearly as ominous as renderings of the Devil himself. Members of the clergy often urged resistance to the Commune sometimes at the pain of eternal damnation. Meanwhile, the rich bourgeoisie and powerful government officials were united in their hatred for the events unfolding in France's traditional capital. From the Russian Czar to the London businessman, the elites of Europe clamored for the destruction of, what *The Times* called, this predominance of "Labour over Capital."

Fall of the Paris Commune

The end of the Commune was inevitable. Its only hope would have been to win over the rest of France to its cause. Given that most of the French populace consisted of peasants, and peasants who had recently chosen a monarchist majority in elections to the Assembly, national support of the Commune was never really conceivable. Although the Commune had a trained military force and the advantage of a heavily fortified city, the military advantage shifted daily to Versailles as soldiers were released by Bismarck from prisoner of war camps and peasant youth were trained to fight.

At the beginning of April, French regulars advanced on Paris. By May 1, the artillery of the Versailles government began to shell the capital. After three weeks of bitter fighting, government troops entered Paris on May 21 after a gate was betrayed. For a week thereafter, radical Communards delayed the final triumph of reaction with bloody street fighting. Barricades were erected throughout Paris and, particularly in the working class districts, the bitter fight lasted until resistance was impossible. When on May 28 the last barricade fell, much of Paris was in ruins. Fires had been set to delay the advance of the Versailles troops and even more were caused by the fighting. The French government, in its hunger to reassure the powerful, had done more damage to Paris than any invading army before or since.

But more than bricks and buildings were destroyed. The victorious government troops practiced a type of savage repression unthinkable even by their most embittered opponents. Although the records are imprecise, upwards of 25,000 individuals—men, women and children—were killed after the fall of the Commune by the triumphant government troops. Dispassionate observers ranging from British reporters to American diplomats were stunned by the viciousness of the repression. The troops were both brutal and capricious. There was neither so much as a pretense of trials nor concern for the victims' possible innocence. Men were shot for no other reason than that they had the well worn hands of manual laborers. Women and children were executed on the slightest suspicion of Communard sympathies evidenced, in many cases, by the threadbare working class clothes on their bodies. Although some argued these excesses were the product of overly-excited and poorly trained soldiers, members of the left saw the massacres as a type of class revenge against the common people who had dared defy Versailles.

Significance of the Commune

Appraising the Commune in terms of immediate effects, one would have to declare it was not just a failure but a setback. After all, the repression the Commune sparked was, in the words of Thiers, "to bleed democracy white for a generation." Not only in France but throughout Europe, the years immediately following the fall of the Commune were to be bleak for the revolutionary left. Thousands killed, scores exiled to Devil's Island and countless terrified survivors were to be part of the Commune's legacy. The entire experiment in Paris could easily be regarded as a disaster for revolutionaries.

Yet, it is inaccurate to see the Commune's legacy in solely negative terms. In as much as the Commune had been a break with the conventional wisdom of the existing order, it was a great success. Despite its short life span and the fierce reaction it spawned, the Paris Commune was to inspire generations of leftists. The Commune's attempts at grass roots democracy and workers' control of society were components of a larger dream which has become part of revolutionary legend. However fleetingly it existed, the Commune offered the hope that one day a new society would be born. For Marx and Engels, it was the prototype of the future workers state, while V.I. Lenin (1870–1924) stressed the sense of liberation felt by the common people during this brief "festival of the oppressed."

For Marx, Engels, Lenin, and many others in the revolutionary left, the decisive lesson of the Commune was the need to smash the existing state apparatus. Many movements, before and after, thought it sufficient to replace "evil" rulers with "good" rulers. What the Commune accomplished, instead, was a transformation of the entire structure of government in order to achieve democratic aspirations. Thereafter, it would be a watchword of revolutionaries that the existing state must be smashed. That the Commune was the product of the very specific features of France's defeat in the Franco-Prussian war mattered little to future radicals. As so often in history, the myth would prove more powerful than the reality.

2. Birth and Development of Left Radicalism after 1871

The subjugation of the Paris Commune quieted the hopes of revolutionaries for an immediate European uprising. Meanwhile in Great Britain, a number of new laws including giving a larger number of men the right to vote, had pushed many onto the path of legal reform. Where conditions were most exploitative for workers, as in Italy and Spain, the low level of industrial development kept the proletariat in a weakened position.

By contrast, rapid industrialization had given Germany a robust labor movement with avowed revolutionary goals. Even here, however, the success of Bismarck in unifying Germany had invigorated nationalism to the point where there were no immediate prospects for a successful revolutionary project. Thus in the conditions of the 1870s, it is not surprising that much of the effort of the European left went into more modest day-to-day organizing ventures.

Rise of the Trade Unions

Revolutionaries in nineteenth-century Europe devoted themselves to more than grand transcontinental enterprises like the First International or radical insurrections like the Commune. They worked to build up organizations of workers which could both fight for material improvements (higher wages, shorter hours, better working conditions) and prepare proletarians to take power in the future. Although the origins of trade unions can be traced backed to the medieval guilds, unionism took on a new importance in the period after 1871. The growth of unionism can be linked with broad developments largely outside the movement's control: 1) the economic cycle, 2) technological and social changes, 3) political developments, and 4) the relative strength of employers and workers both organizationally and ideologically.

When conditions of widespread unemployment and economic downturn existed, trade unions were inevitably taxed to the limits of their strength, if not crushed. Having no control over the boom or bust nature of the economy, workers often despaired of union activity, let alone strikes, feeling their positions hopeless in face of ever changing providence. As the economy improved and employment rose, so did the prospects for unionism. Likewise, the rapid introduction of technological change could render entire groups of workers powerless. Hand weavers serve as one often cited example, for these workers saw their craft skills replaced by machines in a matter of a few years. Yet, once workers became acclimated to the new technology, their self confidence returned.

Nor was the political system an impartial spectator standing on the sidelines of industrial conflict. Governments throughout Europe actively helped the bourgeoisie accumulate capital and, hence, control its work force. As a result, worker's rights were often severely restricted with unions outlawed or, at a minimum, prohibited from striking for much of the nineteenth century. Thus, wherever trade unionism developed in Europe, it always did so with a keen eye cast upon the political system and how it could be altered to level the playing field between the bourgeoisie and the laborers. In addition, the conflict between laborers and the bourgeoisie was fought on the level of ideas as well. That is, the capitalists sought to convince workers that theirs was the "best of all possible worlds" while radicals created an alternative world view.

Given these inherent difficulties, trade unions never succeeded in organizing more than a fraction of those who toiled for wages. With the possible exception of Great Britain, unionism operated more on the margins rather than in the heart of large scale industry. Trade union members were most likely highly skilled workers employed in small to medium enterprises. Given that the working class was far from homogenous, even within a given country, what organizations that did exist were usually local or, at best, regional. Trade unions often rejected strikes either for ideological reasons or because they had no opportunity of winning a direct confrontation with the bourgeoisie. By the mid-1870s, a recession hit much of Western Europe with the resulting increase in unemployment rendering most unions ineffective where they were not crushed completely. Yet by the end of the nineteenth century, the diverse and often hostile segments of the European working class began to come together, often under at least nominally revolutionary leadership.

As industrial capitalism expanded and, in turn, restructured the labor process, it radically altered the lives of average people. One response to the devastating economic and social subordination so many workers experienced was socialist trade unionism. Trade unions offered a pragmatic way of collectively advancing, or at least defending, proletarian interests in a way that individual efforts could not. With the rise of industrial capitalism, a laborer's skills, which traditionally had protected workers' living standards, became less important. As a result, many workers turned to unionism. That is, many a worker who once could count on his skill to guarantee both steady employment and a living wage, now turned to collective organization for help.

Unlike the United States, these unions were socialist and frequently revolutionary in their perspective. This is largely because socialism provided a framework which allowed the average person to understand and interpret the tensions and conflicts of industrial society. Thus, on both the practical and the ideological level, trade unions were to become an indispensable part of organized resistance to capitalist society. This is exemplified by the fact that the majority of trade unions were typically associated with a radical political party. In Germany, the Social Democratic Party had, in fact, created the so-called Free Trade Unions. Across the Rhine river in France, the national trade union federation, *Confédération Générale du Travail* (CGT), was associated with the doctrine of revolutionary syndicalism. Even in relatively moderate Great Britain, the unions were socialist in outlook and instrumental in the creation of the Labour Party. Unions were to bring the class struggle onto the factory floor while the party waged war throughout the rest of society.

The last two decades of the nineteenth century saw a steady and rapid rise in the number of unionized workers. A look at three of the most important nations of Europe shows unheard of gains for the trade union movement during this period. Witness the following numbers. In Great Britain, the first nation to have an industrial revolution, there existed 674,000 union members in 1887. A mere five years later, in 1892, union membership had soared to over a million and a half, while in 1905, 1,997,000 people carried union cards. And this escalation was not limited to the island nation which first transformed itself into an industrial capitalist society.

Across the channel on the continent of Europe, the increases were just as striking. In France, despite the relatively slow pace of industrialization and the continuing preponderance of the peasantry, there were 139,000 trade unionists in 1890. This figure more than doubled in three years, for by 1893 there were 402,000 union members. In 1902, less than a decade later, the total had reached 614,000. Meanwhile, the rapid industrialization of the newly united German Empire would result in even more spectacular growth. From the relatively low number of 95,000 workers enrolled in trade unions in 1887, German union membership had skyrocketed to 294,000 by 1890. This swift expansion continued into the twentieth century with 887,000 workers belonging to unions by 1903.

As always is the case with statistics, these numbers say little in and of themselves. But they are indicative of the growth of a mass base for anticapitalist politics among the European working class. Further, growing union membership was accompanied by waves of intensive labor struggles and massive industrial conflicts. Not only did more strikes take place, the whole character of the trade union movement changed during the last decades of the century. Trade unions moved from being largely passive self-help organizations to active confrontational vehicles for improving the lot of their membership. Their struggles increasingly were seen as not only for immediate concessions but also as part of a revolutionary process. That is not to say that all or even most trade unionists were revolutionary. Still, they overwhelmingly saw themselves as some type of opponent to capitalism.

Besides numerical growth, what changes took place in European labor in the later part of the 1800s? Not only more workers, but different types of workers joined unions. Much of the boost in membership came from the organization of previously non-unionized labor. Proletarians such as dock workers, miners, gas workers and transportation workers joined organized labor. What all of these trades had in common, besides their previous non-union status, was that they were in key sectors of the industrial economy. Therefore, a strike within in any one of these industries could have huge repercussions. After all, miners and gas workers provided the energy that drove the industrial economy, while dock workers and other transportation workers were vital to the flow of goods and services.

During this same period, hundred of thousands, if not millions, of women were forced by economic necessity to work outside of the home. During the 1880s and 1890s, something like a third of all females over ten years of age worked outside their households in Great Britain and France while nearly 20% did so in Germany. Although domestic service accounted for a large number of these female workers (there were 2,000,000 domestics in the extreme case of Britain by 1891) women workers labored in textile, clothing and, increasingly, food manufacture. Of course, even these figures understate the extent of female labor, especially since most working class women worked at least part-time (taking in laundry, for example) and all but a fortunate few were occupied with socially necessary but unpaid work in the home. Although still concentrated in typical "female" industries, women began to play an even more important role in the labor movement as both their number and the diversity of their employment grew.

Moreover, the trade unions themselves tended to change. Both through mergers and the birth of new unions, the labor movement at the end of the century looked quite different from the fragmented, craft-oriented organizations of earlier days. As hitherto unorganized workers poured into the trade union movement, the conventional wisdom which held that strikes were usually counterproductive was soon abandoned. While more moderate craft unions would persist, the "new Unionism" would lead to, in the twentieth century, the development of mass industrial unions. In these unions, all members of a plant belonged to the same union, instead of being divided across numerous craft lines.

This change within the trade unions was heavily influenced by a number of trendsetting strikes such as the London dock strike of 1889. These strikes would arouse many workers to the possibility, if not necessity, of both trade union organization and militant actions in the workplace. These battles were not purely a matter of "bread and butter" although such routine issues were obviously important. In many instances, particularly in certain nations like Germany, strikes helped to satisfy the thirst for action which had been dammed up by years of despotism. Many German workers, for instance, failed to make much differentiation between strikes and unions, on the one side, and the social revolution's political expression—Social Democracy—on the other. (Social Democracy was the name of the political party of the workers.) Even where the root cause of strikes was most clearly economic, many saw the conflict in terms of a struggle for power. That is, numerous workers often felt "Strike today, Revolution tomorrow!" Of course, then, like now, public opinion could change rapidly. Yesterday's revolutionary could be today's loyal employee and back again to revolutionary next week. Except for a hardened cadre of revolutionaries, the mood of the masses changed as circumstances shifted.

Nonetheless, among workers there was a clear shift to the left during the 1880s and 1890s. The economic liberalism of authors like Adam Smith (1723–1790) had grown largely out of favor if it had ever been in favor, with the unpropertied mass of the European populace. If there was an "invisible hand of the market," it certainly was not on the side of the common people. While religion had once served as the "heart of a heartless world," many workers sought new ways of explaining the world as it was. Socialism, especially Marxism, was attractive to such workers as an ideology which could both explain contemporary problems and offer alternatives for the future. While very few workers read *Das Kapital*, millions became familiar—however imprecisely—with certain key Marxian concepts like "the labor theory of value," "all history is the history of class struggle," and "workers of the world, unite." These ideas were the subject of countless articles in the labor press and articulated in hundreds of thousands of radical speeches. Eventually, political parties throughout the European continent were to carry these and other ideas to ever growing numbers of proletarians.

Creation of Socialist Political Parties

While struggles intensified in the workplace, workers began to look again at politics as a means to improve their condition. Preexisting radical and republican hatreds of the "rich" and the "plutocracy" intensified after 1871. The bitter ordeal of industrialization ultimately convinced many, particularly manual workers, of the injustice of the social order. As workers felt increasingly distant from the world of the bourgeoisie, the idea of class-based political parties gained wider acceptance. In other words, political parties began to be formed which claimed to represent a certain social group in society rather than claiming to speak for the entire nation. In England, the Labour Party, as the name suggests, saw itself as presenting working people while the Tories, or conservatives, maintained they represented all Englishmen. Segregated in their proletarian districts (ghettos) like Wedding in Berlin or West Ham in London, workers viewed political issues, such as the fight for extension of voting rights, from the perspective of proletarians, not just citizens.

As even the most modest property qualification for voting would disenfranchise many working men (few in power yet envisioned giving women the vote), workers overwhelmingly became proponents of universal suffrage—at least for male citizens. (Radicals were far less likely to share such anti-female prejudice as shown by the immense success of *Woman Under Socialism* written by August Bebel [1840–1913] and published in 1883 which went through 50 German and 15 foreign language editions by 1914.) Where all men were not able to vote, there were massive struggles such as the enormous general strike in Belgium in 1892, which demanded an expansion of the franchise. Since governments were national in scope, any effort to pressure them had to likewise be national if it were to have any hope of success. Thus, the very organization of national states in Europe helped push the working class in each country toward the formation of national, class-based parties. These parties were typically called "socialist" or "social democratic"—in fact, the two words were considered interchangeable in the nineteenth century.

The most powerful of these parties was to be the Social Democratic Party of Germany (SPD) formed in 1875 by the combination of two hitherto hostile groupings: the state socialist Lassalleans who attempted to collaborate with the government and the Marxist-oriented Eisenachers who were part of the IWMA. Despite attempts to destroy this party with a series of repressive laws enacted by the German Reichstag in 1878, the Social Democrats, under the leadership of August Bebel and Wilhelm Liebknecht (1826–1900), were to become an "empire within an empire." This is certainly true if election results are any indication. Starting with less than 125,000 votes in 1871, the SPD would gather over 500,000 in 1884. Six years later, in 1890, over one million German men cast their ballots for the Social Democrats while this figure doubled to over 2,000,000 votes by 1898.

Not merely an election machine, the German Social Democrats furthermore possessed a press empire. By the end of the nineteenth century, the SPD had 75 papers of which over half were dailies. Besides their theoretical journal *Die Neue Zeit* (the New Age) which advanced Marxist theory, there were a surprising number of non-political publications affiliated with the party. Among the latter were various special interest publications many with a circulation over 100,000. Thus, a radical intellectual could spend the evening perusing the pages of *Die Neue Zeit* while less theoretically oriented workers could spend their free time with *Der Arbeiter Radfahrer* (Worker Cyclist) or the *Arbeiter Turnzeitung* (Worker Gymnastic Newspaper.) Even socialist innkeepers and stenographers had their own publications.

The party created an entire alternative world for their supporters.

If a worker wanted to borrow a novel, there were worker libraries. Those who wished to sing could join "red" singing societies. For those who enjoyed beer, there were frequent meetings and dinners in beer halls while those with a drinking problem could join the German Workers Temperance Federation—a sort of socialist Alcoholics Anonymous. All these activities served a number of important functions. They created a sense of belonging—a group solidarity among socialist workers who otherwise might have been isolated or demoralized. Meanwhile, the party press and the seemingly countless SPD-sponsored activities served to form an information network where issues could be discussed and news exchanged. Thus, a night at the local biergarten might allow debate on controversial party proposals, be a place for a member to find out about possible job openings from comrades, or just drink and have fun. Finally, all the efforts of the Social Democrats aimed at reinforcing the class consciousness that industrial capitalism had first created.

All Social Democrats were not content to limit their agitation to only economic or more traditional "worker" issues. Even topics as controversial as sexuality and sexual preference drew the attention of some in the party. Thus, when Oscar Wilde was arrested on a morals charge for homosexual activity in 1895, an article in *Die Neue Zeit* defended the Irish author and decried the "arbitrary moral concepts" which had led to his detention. Of course, most socialists were loath to add gay rights to their already lengthy list of demands. Still, in 1898, from his seat in the Parliament, August Bebel openly championed a petition to legalize homosexual relations between consenting adults over sixteen years of age.

Yet even in Germany, where not all workers voted for the Social Democrats let alone belonged to the party, there still developed a remarkable identification of the proletariat with the socialist political parties. So much so that an election analyst in one central German district before the First World War expressed amazement that "only" 88% of workers voted for the SPD. Germany may have been one of the most extreme cases in regards to worker's allegiance to socialist parties, but the SPD was far from the only socialist party to be born and grow up in the last decades of the nineteenth century.

Pablo Iglesias (1850–1925), who was to be the first socialist in the Spanish parliament, helped form the Spanish Social Democratic Party in 1879 as a similar party was born in Denmark in the same year. By 1882, France's Parti Ouvrier was organized by Jules Guesde (1845–1922) and five years thereafter a Norwegian Social Democratic Party began. In 1888, socialist political parties were established in both Switzerland and the Austro-Hungarian Empire followed the next year by a new party in Sweden. The Social Democratic Federation in The Netherlands was also formed in 1889. Finally in 1893, the birthplace of industrial capitalism, Great Britain, witnessed the formation of the Independent Labour Party by Keir Hardie (1856–1915) and other socialists.

While other socialist parties could not match the level of electoral success enjoyed by the German party, they were, nonetheless, steadily growing in popularity among the masses. By 1897, the Italian Socialists were to receive 135,000 votes while the Austrian Social Democrats won about 600,000 votes that same year. In 1898, socialists in France saw over 750,000 ballots cast for their candidates while by the end of the century there were thirty-one socialists in the Belgium parliament.

Each party was fashioned within the traditions of its nation and heavily influenced by the leaders who gave it direction. Thus, the French or Spanish parties would lack the iron discipline and significant Marxist influence of the Austrian or German parties, while the British Labour Party would look as much to the work of Robert Owen (1771–1858), a utopian socialist, or the Chartists, who thought universal suffrage would solve labor problems, as to the *Communist Manifesto*. Even the most "orthodox" Marxist parties would, in reality, develop their own manner of functioning in response to the conditions existing at any given time. Thus, it is important to understand that these socialist parties were far from being copies of some grand model or each other. If each organization was so different in so many important ways, how can they be discussed as part of a common movement?

First, all the socialist parties which developed in the late nineteenth century saw themselves as part of a broader, international movement. It was this identification which would lead to them to create a Socialist International in 1889. Further, for all their dissimilarities, these parties held certain fundamental beliefs in common. All believed in working towards a socialist society which would be based on democracy and equality. Further in contrast to non-socialist democrats, they believed in economic democracy and equality which, to them, meant the socialization of the means of production. That is, the socialists believed in the right to vote but also the right to eat. They felt that political democracy was essential but so was a social equality which would ensure that no one lacked the basic human necessities such as food, housing and health care. As much as their individual notions of socialism might diverge, these organizations shared a conviction in the socialist future. Under the careful eye of the scholar, these parties might appear quite different, but to their members such nuances were of little regard.

Further, these parties shared a collective agreement on specific approaches to their socialist goal. For instance, they agreed that they should focus on political activity to promote the cause of labor. This emphasis on politics defined socialists as very distinctive from those who rejected politics, like the anarchists, people who preached self-help like the cooperative movement or the various and sundry Christian groups who promoted faith in the hereafter. At first glance, the use of revolutionary rhetoric seems incompatible with the socialist fidelity to electoral politics. But, the nineteenth century European socialists saw no contradiction in promoting revolution while campaigning for votes. To understand why they felt this way, it is important to comprehend the underlying assumption which these parties shared about the imminent unfolding of industrial capitalism. European socialists believed that as capitalism continued to develop there would exist only two important social classes within society. These would be an ever smaller, if powerful, bourgeoisie and an ever growing working class which would make up the vast majority of the populace. What had been a major class, the peasantry, was viewed as historically doomed. The mechanization of agriculture, socialists believed, would force the peasants from the land as they were no longer needed in any significant number.

Since workers were, according to the socialists, "naturally" drawn to socialism, they would ultimately elect solid left majorities to every national parliament. These majorities would change the political and legal system democratically, while in the factories the trade unions would wrestle control of the economy from the hands of the capitalists. This two edged assault could only be blunted if the rulers violated democratic rights—an option which the vast proletarian masses were thought capable of preventing, if necessary, by means of a general strike.

Although this view may appear hopelessly naive, the rapid pace of industrialization meant a constantly growing portion of the population was made up of workers. The vast numbers of workers, combined with the democratization of Europe throughout the nineteenth century, seemed to make this theory, at the time, self-evident. The socialist parties did not foresee the continued persistence of the peasantry and the middle classes nor did they realize the full potential of the upper classes to turn to repression. The twentieth century was to demonstrate that democracy was not irreversible: witness Mussolini in Italy, Hitler in Germany, Franco in Spain and Stalin (1879–1953) in Russia. Thus, socialist parties saw themselves as the representatives of the workers who would inevitably become the vast majority in nation after nation. Once this majority was achieved, political democracy would allow the revolutionary transformation of society.

Since they realized that this revolutionary process would not take place only within one nation, socialists felt they should coordinate their efforts across national boundaries. Leading socialist theorists including Karl Marx, Karl Kautsky (1854–1938) and Leon Trotsky (1879–1940) not only expected an international revolution, they deemed it essential if socialism was to succeed. After all, if the capitalist class was becoming more and more international in nature, why not the working class? This belief led to the establishment of a Second (or Socialist) International in 1889 which was to be much stronger and much different from the earlier International Working Men's Association.

Founding of the Second International

On 14 July 1889, the 100th anniversary of the storming of the Bastille during the French Revolution, two international meetings took place in Paris. In one hall sat representatives of English trade unions and moderate French socialists. In another, a gathering of socialists from the European continent who considered themselves, more or less Marxist. All the same, the lines were often not so clearly drawn between the two rival radical groups. In many cases, the decision as to which congress to attend was dictated more by personal attachments or feuds than by any clear ideological affinity. Often delegates attempted to attend meetings of both groups while anarchists enthusiastically tried to disrupt both groupings. Out of this organizational competition and chaos, the Marxist-oriented group emerged more popular, as many delegates defected from the more moderate and eclectic gathering to join with the continental socialists.

In actuality, the Marxist meeting was the more broad-based of the two, with 391 delegates representing twenty countries throughout Europe and even including four people from the United States. Among those in attendance were many of the most prominent European socialists. The past heritage of the International Working Men's Association was assured symbolic continuity with the appearance of Eleanor Marx, daughter of Karl Marx, and her two French brothers-in-law. The German delegation included Wilhelm Liebknecht and August Bebel, the only men not to vote for war credits during the Franco-Prussian War, as well as Clara Zetkin (1857–1933), the socialist-feminist leader of radical working women. Great Britain supplied a celebrated artist in the person of William Morris while the Austrian delegation was chaired by Dr. Viktor Adler (1852–1918), a Viennese doctor of considerable intellectual authority.

Like the IWMA a quarter century before, this International Workers' Congress was to be of much greater significance symbolically than practically. For example, much time was wasted by protracted discussions over who was an accredited delegate and who was not. This problem arose because unlike the First International, the Socialist International was to be composed of socialist parties and bona fide trade unions. Accordingly, argument raged over who was and who was not a "genuine" representative from a "bona fide" association. In fact, most of the first two days of the gathering were wasted in squabbles over who was entitled to vote. After this process was completed and various anarchists, who jumped up on tables to denounce meeting organizers as traitors, were expelled, the congress did make progress. For three days, the delegates heard reports on the socialist movement in the different countries represented. This interchange of information helped eliminate the isolation many socialists had felt since the fall of the Commune.

Not that this was all that was accomplished. After the reports, the delegates next took up the question of the type of international labor standards for which they ought to fight. Of course, this was a matter which greatly concerned the average worker. The socialists went on record in favor of the eight hour day and improved working conditions. A resolution about peace was adopted which condemned standing armies and urged their replacement with a "people in arms" while contending that socialism would abolish the threat of war forever. Since, as previously noted, socialists believed in the power of democracy, it is not surprising that the congress resolved to fight for universal male suffrage wherever it did not exist.

The Socialist International and May Day

To push for these demands, particularly the eight-hour day, it was decided that May 1, should be the occasion for worldwide workers protests which would demonstrate the power of the new International. This day had become symbolic for radicals since 1886 when labor protests in Chicago led to a deadly confrontation with the police during which an unknown individual threw a bomb into the crowd. Eight police officers and an unknown number of workers were killed by the explosion and the resulting police cross fire. In an atmosphere of hysteria whipped up by the press against the "scum of Europe," eight anarchist labor organizers were prosecuted for conspiracy to commit murder. All defendants were found guilty and four were sent to the gallows. Another committed suicide, while the remaining three were pardoned in 1893 by Illinois Governor John Peter Altgeld (1847–1902), who denounced the trial as a criminal farce.

On the final day of the meeting which launched the Second International, it was resolved: "A great manifestation will be organized … simultaneously in all countries and in all towns … workers will call upon the public authorities to reduce the working day by law to eight hours and to put the other resolutions of the Congress of Paris into effect. In view of the fact that a similar manifestation has already been decided on for May 1, 1890, by the American Federation of Labor at its Congress held at St. Louis in December 1888, this date is adopted for the international manifestation." From the start, this bold resolution was to be the source of disagreement within the new International. More radical socialists felt May Day should be a time for work stoppages and militant demonstrations whereas the more cautious were content to hold public meetings after working hours. In fact, the German delegation had insisted on adding to the resolution that each party would honor May Day "under the conditions imposed on them by the particular situation in each country."

Of course, resolutions on paper mean little if they are not acted upon. So, the proof of the radical movement's strength would be disclosed in 1890. Would the socialist parties represented at the birth of the Second International actually be able to produce impressive mass backing for this resolution? Despite endless disagreements over implementation, the European left almost universally welcomed the idea of May Day protests.

When May 1, 1890 came even the most pessimistic were overwhelmed by the size and spirit of the demonstrations. While it was not astonishing that there were widespread work stoppages in France, strikes also broke out in Austria, Hungary, Belgium, The Netherlands, and Scandinavia as well as in Italy and Spain. By way of contrast, the British Trade Unions avoided strikes and held their mass meeting on

May 4. Even so, the rally held in London's Hyde Park attracted well over 250,000 people ranging from dockers in their rough clothes to working women dressed in their finest apparel. Likewise, the German SPD thought it unwise to provoke the government and tried to avoid work stoppages. Despite pleas from party officials against "an undue show of spirit," 40,000 workers in the port city of Hamburg stayed away from work.

Even the relatively tame protests made in Great Britain and Germany were not without effect as many marveled at the size of the demonstrations. The success of the May Day demonstrations gave the Second International a virtually mythical power in millions of eyes. What began on 1 May 1890 was to become an institution for the European left. On one level, May Day protests were little more than the demand for a labor day holiday, yet on another, they were a custom which asserted working class internationalism and inspired the average laborer to feel part of a powerful worldwide movement. For instance, a previously apolitical clay miner told a story which may not be completely atypical. First learning of the Second International's May Day call from an article in the socialist *Pfälzischer Post*, he rushed to his fellow workers and announced: "You're all skipping work today … It's the First of May and hundreds of thousands of workers throughout the world are taking off work and protesting the tyrannical yoke that they suffer under." Word spread among the clay miners who had a wagon of beer and food brought into the nearby woods where three hundred workers proceeded to have an impromptu May Day celebration. That the tiny seed of a news article could so quickly bloom into a spontaneous May 1 demonstration showed how fertile the soil was among the lower class.

No International Socialist Congress would be called in 1890. The next gathering was held in Brussels in August 1891 where 337 delegates represented fifteen different countries. Immensely heartened by the success of May Day in 1890 and 1891, this congress resolved to make it an annual event while adding the demand for continued peace between nations to the official list of demands. This time the International took the opportunity to call for a labor standstill on May

1. Although this resolution was to apply to supporters throughout the world, there remained an escape hatch for the more timid or vulnerable. Thus, the final resolution called for strikes on May Day "everywhere except where it is impracticable." These varied approaches to May Day signal differences within the International which would later escalate and finally lead to its destruction in 1914.

In addition to divisions within the ranks of the socialists, the Brussels congress had to deal once more with the disruption of anarchists. Although only a small number were able to obtain credentials from trade unions to attend and those individuals were easily voted down, the anarchists continued to be a source of agitation to the Socialist International. Even if anarchists could be refused admittance when they came from openly hostile organization or thinly disguised front groups, there was a problem when they arrived with mandates from trade unions. This was not a problem for countries like Great Britain or Germany which had highly disciplined union movements. However, in many nations, like France, Italy and Spain, there were rival union organizations, each based on different political and ideological perspectives.

Since the socialists had no wish to alienate the unions which were such a critical part of their overall revolutionary strategy, they had no choice but to suffer the occasional anarchist from Italy or even some English unionists who remained wedded to the Liberal Party. Unlike the later Communist International, the Second International was never a purely Marxist organization. Further, the socialists who were the mainstay of the International had no real desire to transform it into a Communist organization. Members of the Second International regarded the organization as the overall framework in which radical parties could unite the entire working class. Since this class naturally had diverse levels of consciousness and varying political beliefs, socialist parties and their International made every attempt to accommodate these differences. This conception is far removed from that of revolutionaries in the twentieth century who felt purity of doctrine was primary. If the Communist motto in the twentieth century was to be, in Lenin's words, "Better fewer but better," the nineteenth century socialists felt, despite their exasperation with the anarchists, "The more, the merrier."

Women Workers and Socialism

Thus, far, the revolutionary left has been discussed almost exclusively in terms of men. In fact, by the close of the nineteenth century, women played a vital role within European radicalism. Throughout Europe, different strata of society increasingly came forward with demands that women be granted equal rights and opportunities. While socialists agreed with the moral arguments made by middle class feminists that the suppression of females was unjust, they had a distinctive theory on the question of women. For the left, in the words of Clara Zetkin, "the question of women's emancipation is, in the end, the question of women's work."

That is, leftists argued that the oppression of women was rooted within the needs of a class stratified economic system. If the institution of private property had dictated the domination of women by men, then women working outside of the home would be a precondition for women gaining equal rights. In both the writings of socialist feminists like Zetkin and Marxist men like August Bebel and Frederick Engels, there was a common theme. The working class man cannot be free if he continues to oppress the working class woman. Remember, they considered this more than a question of morality or "doing the right thing." For the nineteenth century revolutionary, the oppression of women was but one aspect of a system which, after abolition, would provide freedom and equality for all peoples.

By the closing decades of the nineteenth century, the Marxist prediction of growing female participation in the labor force seemed to be coming true. Ever greater numbers of women were seeking work outside the home in all the industrialized nations of Europe. Once in the factory or work shop, the woman worker was exploited even more intensely than her male counterpart, as female laborers repeatedly received only half (or less than half) of the wages a man was paid for the same work. In addition, unlike men, women had no political rights. They could neither run for public office nor vote for those who could. In some countries, there were even prohibitions on women attending political meetings.

As more lower class women entered the industrial work force, they frequently found neither their male co-workers nor middle class feminist "ladies" of much help. The former saw them as unwanted competition for jobs and a downward pressure on wages, while the latter were preoccupied with achieving equality within the existing order. Workers seldom followed the high-minded words of Bebel in *Women Under Socialism*, while middle class women's issues, like female admittance to medical schools, were not a burning concern for factory females. Therefore, working women struggled to build their own unions and organizations—but typically within the general orbit of the socialist movement.

If this failure to build exclusively feminist organizations seems strange, bear in mind that the socialist movement offered one of the few places in a male dominated society where women could develop their abilities. Further, for all the sexism which remained among male workers, the socialists promised a revolutionary transformation of society which would require a new equality among the sexes. Interestingly enough, the choice for the bulk of European women was not between socialism and feminism. The real choice was between revolutionary politics and religion. Fighting against the rising tide of secularism, the churches, particularly the Roman Catholic Church, sought to maintain, if not expand, their female base. The Roman Catholic Church postured as the defender of traditional women's rights and attempted to pit pious wife against atheistic husband. The dramatic growth in full-time female church personnel, the Papacy's encouragement of the cult of the Virgin Mary, and the creation of additional female saints were all attempts to incorporate women into "holy mother church."

As the number of working women increased so did their self confidence. A strike by "match girls" at London match factories in 1888 resulted in a modest pay increase, for instance. More and more women became members of trade unions although these women remained a minority of the female labor force. Still, trade unionism, which had been almost an exclusively male institution a generation before, began to have significant, if small, numbers of women involved. By 1913, the year before World War I, most industrial countries could boast women within the organized labor movement. Their percentage of trade union membership ranged from a modest number in some countries (5% in Sweden) to a somewhat more substantial figure in others (9% in Germany, 10.5% in Great Britain, and 12.3% in Finland.) Regardless of their precise percentage, trade unionism was poised for an explosive influx of female members that would occur soon after the beginning of the First World War. Likewise, the small single digit percentage of women in the socialists parties would grow into huge figures after the war had ended.

By the 1890s the "Woman Question" was firmly on the socialist agenda, and female workers were demanding to be heard within radical organizations. Accordingly, during the 1896 London congress of the Second International, thirty socialist female delegates gathered to discuss their common concerns. These women, who came from a number of different nations of Europe including Germany, Great Britain, Belgium and Holland, fought for the socialist parties to increasingly address the needs of women in order to draw them into the revolutionary movement. These efforts would ultimately result in moving a number of women's concerns, like the right to vote and equal pay for equal work, into the forefront of the socialist agenda.

Anarchism

Having discussed the woman's movement inside socialism, it is fitting to address another element inside the movement. Anarchism, like socialism, democracy, freedom or any other abstract concept, is a doctrine which defies simple definition. This is particularly true for anarchism, as it was based on an extreme emphasis on the individual. Therefore, unlike Marxists, there exists no central body of thought, let alone organization, to which all anarchists subscribe. In general, however, anarchism in the nineteenth century rejected all political authority and, thereby, any participation in elections. Furthermore, anarchists had as their goal the elimination of any state or government, hoping to replace such structures with a self-regulated society of individuals.

While all anarchist theory rests on the intellectual basis of nineteenth century liberalism, there was a clear dividing line between those anarchists who believed in private property (in the late twentieth century, these people will call themselves "libertarians") and those who rejected private ownership as a source of social inequality. It was the latter, alternatively called libertarian socialists, anarcho-communists, or socialist anarchists, which was to be important in the European revolutionary movement—and in giving the socialists so many headaches.

Under the influence of the Russian theorist and activist, Michael Bakunin (1814–1876), anarchism first emerged in the 1860s as a serious rival to Marxism within the left. The struggles between Marx and the socialists, on the one hand, and Bakunin and the anarchists, on the other, contributed in large measure to the ultimate failure of the International Working Men's Association. Bakunin championed the violent expropriation of capitalist property and the establishment of a collectivist society without any intermediate transitional stage. Yet, it was far more than disputes over abstractions that made the anarchists and the socialists such bitter opponents within the revolutionary left.

Although few actually practiced it, anarchists believed in, or at a minimum defended, "propaganda of the deed," a doctrine which held that talking about oppression, organizing protest meetings, or voting in elections all wasted time. What was needed, argued the anarchists, was an illustration to the downtrodden of the weakness of the system. What better demonstration then the assassination of prominent members of the state like czars, kings, and presidents? By employing terrorism against the bourgeoisie or their representatives, "propaganda of the deed" was intended to spark popular insurrections. While there were a number of political killings and even more unsuccessful assassination attempts, there were no mass uprisings.

After 1878, anarchist "propaganda of the deed," which had previously been limited to Russia, Italy and Spain, spread throughout Europe. Two unsuccessful attempts were made on the life of Kaiser Wilhelm I (1797–1888) of Germany which gave Bismarck a long-sought excuse to outlaw the socialist movement. That neither of the men who attempted to kill Wilhelm I were Social Democrats nor the fact that the party repeatedly condemned individual acts of terror was of any help to the soon outlawed SPD. This incident nicely illustrates one motivation socialists had for hating anarchism. The Social Democrats, and not only in Germany, viewed anarchists as frustrated petty bourgeois (or small businessmen) and lumpen proletarian (or habitually unemployed) adventurers who provided the police with the justification they sought to repress the left. That is, the socialists saw anarchists as frivolous, if not unstable, individuals who rejected the hard labor necessary to build a revolutionary movement. In the eyes of socialists, the anarchists opted instead for the emotionally satisfying, but inherently counterproductive, path of violence.

Although the vast majority of anarchists personally rejected homicide as a political procedure, few would criticize assassinations. Indeed, "propaganda of the deed" was approved in principle by an Anarchist Congress held in Switzerland in 1879. That the bulk of those attending did so either as a response to the extreme repression existing in Czarist Russia or out of abstract principle made little difference to European socialists or, for that matter, the general public. Anarchism's identification with murder made it easy to brand every lunatic who killed a prominent person with the labels "anarchist" and "revolutionary." Anarchist crimes, real and imagined, prompted the Papal Encyclical *Quod Apostolici Muneris,* which condemned anarchism—and socialism—at the end of 1878.

From the point of view of the police, the numerous assassination attempts and bombings were a welcomed pretext for political repression. In France, for instance, the 1890s saw a large number of crimes committed by men professing to be anarchists. Upon close examination, most of these individuals were merely criminals or madmen with no connection with the anarchist movement and lacking any real understanding of its doctrine. Although there was no evidence of any central "Anarchist conspiracy," the press convinced a large portion of the public otherwise. In addition, as socialists never tired of saying, "propaganda of the deed" was tailored to the needs of the police and repressive governments. In addition to actual acts of violence, the police would sometimes set off a bomb or send an agent provocateur into anarchist circles to stir up trouble. Even now, it is not always possible to say with certainty which actions were committed by genuine anarchists and which were instigated by the police. Once the action was taken, the police could sweep down on whatever radical opponents they wished to arrest.

These political crimes committed or inspired by anarchism were of considerable importance for the socialist movement. Much of the public, as well as many anarchists, made little distinction between anarchism and socialism. Therefore, the socialists received consider-able blame and suffered abundant repression because of anarchist activities. In addition, anarchists frequently denounced revolutionary socialists as traitors because they participated in elections or fought for reforms. While the Second International looked to representative democracy as the path toward a new society, anarchism castigated representative government on principle. How can one man, they asked, really represent another? Moreover, as Marxists were quick to point out, anarchists expressed their scorn for the stupidity of the masses who often used the vote to elect conservatives or even reac-tionaries. Based upon an essentially individualistic world view, many anarchists simply did not believe in democracy. After all, majority rule and representative democracy of necessity limited the liberty of the individual. In essence, the anarchists wanted not political freedom but freedom from politics.

Syndicalism

As repression broke up anarchist groups and popular rejection of violence limited their base of support, some anarchists began to develop an alternative revolutionary strategy. This new doctrine was known as syndicalism. The word "syndicalism" is the English translation of the French term for trade unionism. Syndicalism's goal was to turn unions into revolutionary instruments which would form the basis of the new society. Rather than "propaganda of the deed," syndicalists believed that the revolution would be sparked by a general strike which would paralyze society. During this general strike, the workers would take over the means of production and abolish the state, replacing it with a new society based on workers' organizations. Thus, syndicalism remedied anarchism's glaring problem of organization by a reliance on union structures.

Like anarchism, syndicalism was never a coherent theory as the emphasis was on deed not words. Among key themes, however, was the importance of militancy in the work place including sabotage as a means of struggle and the centrality of rank and file initiative. To prepare for the revolution, syndicalists proclaimed the necessity of organizing unskilled workers while arguing that contracts signed with capitalists need not be honored. By promoting direct action, they felt the class consciousness of workers would be enhanced and the bourgeoisie weakened until the day the general strike signaled the beginning of the revolution. In addition, politics and political parties were scorned as corrupt attempts to compromise with the government and the bourgeoisie. Therefore, the only field of action which mattered was the industrial battlefield. All other campaigns and political activities were at best, to the syndicalists, mere distractions for the working class.

This movement reached its greatest heights in France where the syndicalist *Confédération Générale du Travail* (CGT), founded by an anarchist named Fernand Pelloutier, was to become one of the major trade union federations. Refraining from the more normal union activities like saving funds for pensions, this collection of pugnacious unions devoted itself to direct action. Before the First World War, the *Confédération Générale du Travail* was to play a prominent role in many militant labor struggles including strikes among railroad workers and civil servants. The CGT even attempted to organize soldiers within the French army. Although syndicalism was to have influence in other countries, notably in Spain and Italy, nowhere else was it to achieve such success. Ironically, its emphasis on action was to influence many on the right, most importantly Benito Mussolini (1883–1945), founder of Italian fascism.

Failure of Repression

Throughout the last decades of the nineteenth century, governments looked upon the expanding left-wing movement with alarm. The swelling ranks of the revolutionary left could not merely be ignored. For the more fearful members of Europe's bourgeoisie, even the most commonplace union conflict with an employer was frequently seen as part of a revolutionary conspiracy. Given this fear and a passionate hatred for socialism, big business, and the governments which protected it, sought to curb the "red menace" by any means necessary.

While this sometimes meant concessions which made the life of the average worker more bearable, the stick of repression was used at least as much as the carrot of compromise. Even liberal England massively expanded her repressive apparatus in the years before World War I with the number of police increasing 20% in the last prewar years. This enlargement of the British police force did not occur solely to fight common criminals, but rather, in the words of one police inspector, to combat general unrest "too great for its normal strength."

Repression took many different forms and varied in intensity from place to place. England, for instance, shied away from the outright use of force save for exceptional situations. In contrast, on the other side of Europe, Czarist Russia elevated the whip and Siberian exile to almost a state religious ritual in its drive to curb revolutionaries. Although few European countries were as tolerant as England or as brutal as Russia, all practiced varied forms of suppression to control those who challenged the status quo. If the methods varied, the goals did not.

One universal method of control was the infiltration of radical groups by police spies. This snooping often did not end at a nation's border. Imperial Germany, for example, went so far as to keep tabs on radicals in the United States. In addition, governments would often trade information on revolutionaries. Thus, details of a Russian exile's speech in New York City could wind up in St. Petersburg via Berlin. Likewise, the usually broad-minded British government was always anxious for information concerning anyone of Irish descent—and other nation's agents would gladly provide it.

The problem governments increasingly found was that, except for the anarchists who remained unpredictable, most European revolutionaries worked openly. That is, the spies seldom found out much more than could be gleaned from reading a socialist newspaper like the German *Vorwärts (Forwards)*.

Of course, these spies could also be used as agent provocateurs who would break the law in order to provide a pretense for police action. Even these efforts made little impact outside of the successful disruption of anarchist circles.

When the police or army did attack a radical demonstration, however, the results could be lethal. In 1891 in a small northern French town called Fourmies, a peaceful May Day march was met with rifle fire hitting fifty and killing ten instantly. The following year in Carmaux, France, a miner's strike of 2800 saw the mobilization of 1500 gendarmes (police) and army troops against unarmed workers. In Britain in 1893, the army was sent against striking miners resulting in the "Featherstone Massacre," which left two dead and sixteen wounded. Except for Czarist Russia, the problem which governments had was that the use of force was often counterproductive. True, they could use force to break strikes or halt protests, but the anger the repression unleashed caused far more damage because many previously uncommitted individuals began to sympathize with the left. Until the rise of fascism in the twentieth century, few governments had either the means or the political will to completely crush political opponents.

Anti-Socialist Law in Germany, 1878–1890

The best known and most comprehensive attempt to crush revolutionaries in the nineteenth century was perhaps the anti-socialist law employed by Bismarck in Germany. The law was passed by the Reichstag in 1878 after a press campaign which tried to link the Social Democratic Party with the assassination attempts on Kaiser Wilhelm I. It was, in its time, the most far reaching attempt to crush a radical party. Lasting until 1890, the law forbade all organizations or publications that attempted to subvert the social system or displayed socialist sympathies. The police now had the right to arrest, interrogate and expel suspected socialists. Not only the party but also the affiliated Free Trade Unions were dealt a terrible blow. Thus, many SPD leaders were jailed or forced to flee the country while the socialist press was outlawed and public meetings banned. The only right the SPD retained was the ability to enter elections.

Yet, the party and unions emerged twelve years later stronger than ever because the socialists refused to give up and utilized every means at their disposal to continue their fight. Election campaigns took on added significance as the only legal avenue for radical activity. Free to campaign publicly, German socialists used elections (and, when elected, their parliamentary seats) to crusade for their beliefs. In fact, it was said that the SPD speeches in the Reichstag were given "out the window." That is, they were not intended for other parliament members but for the general public who might be able to read about them in the mainstream press or the parliamentary record.

Further, SPD members built up a clandestine organization which distributed various party publications including the central newspaper *Sozialdemokrat* illegally. Printing their publications in Switzerland or Great Britain, the Social Democrats would then smuggle them into Germany and distribute them among their supporters. This system of distribution was so efficient and successful that it became known as the "red postal service." At the same time, a network of secret agents was organized to hinder government spies. This network became so successful that it ultimately unmasked hundreds of police agents. Later, secret print shops were created within Germany and only the plates were smuggled in from abroad. In 1880, the *Sozialdemokrat* could boast of the thousands of copies distributed "door to door, at factories, in the streets and squares, in omnibuses, and even in churches ... most frightening for the police is that they are very rarely able to find the distributors."

Local party branches were gradually rebuilt under the guise of being apolitical organizations such as choral societies or smokers clubs. Frequently, these "non-political" organizations would even have public meetings where lectures were given on some harmless sounding topic like "The wild birds of central Europe." In reality, the talk would be a coded socialist discourse. (This speaks to the average policeman's lack of imagination for it usually took them some time to see through such transparent ruses.) The work place was not ignored, as every large factory had trusted men who would secretly collect dues and pass on information. Hence, the anti-socialist laws were an abject failure. The German Social Democrats and their counterparts in other nations which suffered repression emerged stronger than ever before. Therefore, as the European left moved towards the twentieth century, an overwhelming sense of optimism prevailed among the revolutionary faithful. An optimism which blinded many to the critical contradictions which were developing within their movement.

3. Splits within the European Left Before World War I

The socialist movement's identification as both revolutionary in its goals and working class in constituency posed difficulties felt increasingly by the 1890s. The movement's talk of revolution and stress on the proletariat made it difficult to win support from other social strata such as the peasantry or the small businessmen. Speeches about the coming socialization of agriculture may have warmed the hearts of many workers but did little to endear the socialists to peasant farmers, who, despite socialist predictions, continued to represent a significant portion of the population. Middle class progressives may have agreed with socialism's immediate reform goals but hesitated to back a movement which sought to totally transform society. Some solid, pragmatic trade unionists felt that revolutionary rhetoric needlessly alarmed employers.

Thus within each European society, there developed a group of reformists who desired to jettison radical theories and change working class-based socialism into a less class specific "people's party." In other words, they thought both the old class-based party model and revolutionary theories were obsolete. These pragmatic politicians argued that the days of revolution were over and that the true goals of socialism could be won gradually through reform legislation and stronger unions. These reformists saw the rising standard of living and increased social welfare laws as evidence against orthodox Marxism, which they felt held back change by needlessly alienating the urban middle class and the peasantry. As socialists expanded their representation in the various parliamentary bodies across Europe, some could not help thinking how many more seats could be theirs if only non-working class and non-revolutionary voters could be reassured. In fact, many legislative seats then held by socialists were only achieved by a small, but vital, crossover by non-proletarian voters.

Further, the growing wealth of working class institutions like unions, combined with relatively high wages for at least some sections of the working populace (the so-called labor aristocracy), produced a material basis for reformist theories. That is, the revolutionary slogan "we shall be all" lost much of its power since many no longer felt "we now are nought." While the economic base for reformism can be overestimated (some groups of highly paid workers remained devoted to revolutionary sentiments), it is important to consider that reformism as a theory only made sense during a period of material advancement. In addition, reformism was strongest in areas where socialists were less concentrated and under heavy pressure from non-socialists, such as in smaller towns or rural areas. The large concentration of workers in cities like Copenhagen, Turin, Berlin or Paris would force such urban areas, in spite of middle class residents, to remain radical "red," while smaller towns might turn reformist "pink."

Revisionist Controversy in Germany

Given its role as the strongest socialist movement in Europe, Germany was the natural place for this new reformist tendency to reveal itself most powerfully. After having survived, and actually prospering, under the anti-socialist law, the German socialists were the envy of most European leftists. Yet, the repression had its effect. During the twelve years of illegality, the party had become more wedded to parliamentarism than ever. Much like their later British counterparts in the Labour Party, the SPD tended to see the world from the vantage point of elected office. Even for those committed to the revolutionary transformation of society, this goal was to be realized by an elected majority in parliament. Years of conflict with anarchists had moved most European socialists farther away from ideas of direct action which they had embraced earlier. Meanwhile, the very concessions they had won from their governments had made revolution appear an increasingly distant, and not always necessary, goal.

Eduard Bernstein (1850–1932) articulated this emerging ideological current. Bernstein, a German socialist, who had lived in exile in
London for a number of years and was greatly influenced by British
gradualism, argued that the revolutionary goal was nothing and the
socialist movement was everything. Although originally a radical
socialist and leading left-wing intellectual, he grew to reconsider his
earlier ideas. Challenging the conceptions of Marx, he rejected the
labor theory of value and asserted that socialism would be achieved
gradually through a long process of reforms. The task of the socialist
movement was, therefore, to fight for worker's political rights and
create proletarian economic organizations, not to dream of revolution.
If immediate reforms could be furthered by cooperation with non-
socialist parties, Bernstein endorsed such measures. His new "revisionist" theory (because it sought to revise Marxism) was first published in *Die Neue Zeit* and later in 1899 as a book known in English as
Evolutionary Socialism.

Bernstein's based his arguments for a reform-oriented, non-
revolutionary party policy on the belief that socialism would be
achieved by the accumulation of piecemeal changes. In addition, he
asserted that sections of the bourgeoisie, particularly small capitalists,
could be won over to support a gradual, democratic, socialist under-
taking. His assumptions were vigorously attacked by those who saw
this view as not only erroneous, but dangerous, as it could lead to the
fragmentation of the radical left. Since the death of Frederick Engels
in 1895 (Karl Marx died in 1883), the European Marxist theorist with
the most intellectual authority had become Karl Kautsky, who became known as the "Pope" of the Second International. It would be
the Austrian-born Kautsky who would lead the attack against
revisionism.

Although Bernstein doubtlessly said what many other socialists
were thinking (and doing), his revisionism caused a major confrontation throughout the European left. For instance, G.V. Plekhanov
(1857–1918), father of Russian Marxism, called the German revisionists "the most vicious enemies of Marxism" while Italy's Antonio

Labriola (1843–1904) severely criticized Bernstein. Meanwhile, V.I. Lenin, leader of the Russian Bolsheviks, would later attack Bernstein in *What is to be Done?* wielding the term "Bernsteinian" as an expression of abuse against those socialists who disagreed with him. The lines which were drawn in this debate would reappear in even sharper contrast during the crisis of the war years.

Kautsky contested the foundation of Bernstein's theories as well as his conclusions. First, he noted that revisionists had distorted Marxist theory by ignoring a number of vital points, including the theory of capitalist crisis which held that the economy would inevitable go from one depression—through a period of relative prosperity—to another depression. Thus, argued Kautsky, Bernstein and his followers had constructed a parody of Marxism and then demolished this imitation. Reformists failed to consider the overall boom-bust nature of the economy, Kautsky contended, and therefore exaggerated the stability of the capitalist economic system by recourse to statistics from only recent years. Particularly unpalatable to Kautsky and other defenders of socialist orthodoxy was Bernstein's insistence on alliance with liberals. In reply, Kautsky argued that the bourgeoisie was becoming more reactionary and even less likely to ally with labor than ever before. At the heart of Kautsky's attacks was the idea that the revisionists wished to abandon class struggle, which would mean the forsaking of not just revolution but socialism itself.

At the Stuttgart Congress of the German Social Democratic Party held in October 1898, the "revisionist" question was a topic of much debate. Following Karl Kautsky among others, the delegates overwhelmingly condemned Bernstein's attack on socialist orthodoxy. At this conference, a young Polish-born woman named Rosa Luxemburg (1870–1919) made her mark by a passionate speech in defense of revolutionary theory. Although then a disciple of Kautsky, Luxemburg was far more committed to revolution than her mentor, as later events would reveal. At the SPD's Hanover Congress held the following year, the woman who was to go on to organize the German Communist Party (KPD) hammered away at the errors of reformism. Along with her close friend and political ally Clara Zetkin, Luxemburg set forth a clear revolutionary perspective on the revisionist controversy.

At the time, however, the lines between the determined revolutionaries and the more moderate "centrist" grouping were blurred at best. The centrists were those who vacillated between the reformist and revolutionary camps—often using revolutionary rhetoric but acting more moderate in practice. After all, Marxism and revolution were part of the German party's heritage. So many party members, who were uncertain revolutionaries at best, sided with the left out of respect for tradition. Other SPD members feared that abandonment of the revolutionary goal would cause the party to lose its identity and fall apart. As fellow reformist Ignaz Auer confided to Bernstein: "My dear Edie, one doesn't formally decide to do what you ask, one doesn't say it, one *does* it."

Thus, Bernstein took a terrible public pounding for his revisionist views. He was assailed not only by Kautsky, defender of the orthodoxy, and Luxemburg, rising leader of the revolutionaries, but also by party founders Wilhelm Liebknecht and August Bebel. An antirevisionist resolution moved by Bebel was passed by a vote of 216 to 21 at the 1899 Hanover Congress. It read, in part, "the development of bourgeois society gives the party no grounds for abandoning or modifying its fundamental views about that society ... the party stand is, as before, that the class struggle must go on." Despite the apparently successful attack on revisionism, the members of the SPD had no inclination to expel Bernstein or his supporters from their party. In the view of the leadership, reformists might be wrong, but they were still part of the working class movement. This stand, so bitterly denounced by Lenin, was consistent with the leadership's conception that the party must represent the entire class while allowing the fullest democracy of opinion. This belief was followed in spite of the fear expressed by Wilhelm Liebknecht, known as the "old soldier of the Revolution," that revisionism "may bring Social Democracy into the camp of the bourgeois parties." The defeat of reformist tendencies within Germany was more apparent than real. The reformists were momentarily quieted but would reappear stronger than ever, particularly with the outbreak of World War I. The debate of reform versus revolution was not limited to the Germans though.

The Millerand Affair in France

Republican France was beset by crisis in 1898. The country was deeply divided over what became known as the Dreyfus affair. Alfred Dreyfus (1859–1935), a Jewish officer in the French army, was accused of selling military secrets to the Kaiser Wilhelm II's (1859–1941) Germany. At first, socialists expressed no interest in the controversy as it was, in their eyes, merely a group of rich militarists accusing a peer. However, it soon became clear that Dreyfus was not only innocent, but was the victim of a frame-up which reached into the highest levels of the French military establishment. That Dreyfus was a scapegoat for anti-Semitic officers became clearer as the crisis worsened. Because an economic crisis contributed to anti-Semitism among sections of the middle class, the elections of 1898 were held against the political backdrop of the Dreyfus controversy. The balloting gave a slender majority to the republican forces including the socialists.

In response, sections of the military, monarchists, anti-Semites, high church officials, and some members of the big bourgeoisie plotted a *coup d'état* against the elected government of the French republic. To organize the broadest possible opposition to this threat, the bourgeois Waldeck-Rousseau government offered the position of Minister of Commerce to a socialist Alexandre Millerand (1859–1943). Millerand accepted, and this broad-based cabinet was able to save the republic. In this position, the erstwhile socialist was able to achieve a number of significant reforms such as introducing secular state education which helped produce a more tolerant younger generation.

Still, this same cabinet included General Gaston Gallifet (1830–1909), as Minister of War, the man whose ruthless repression of Paris in 1871 earned him the title "butcher of the Paris Commune." Gallifets position in the cabinet was enough to make Millerand's decision hard for many to accept. In addition, although this bourgeois government was pro-republic, it was not necessarily prolabor, as its use of the army against strikers in June 1900 illustrated. Obviously, this governmental repression caused a huge predicament for the already fragmented French socialists. Jules Guesde (1845–1922), a rather sectarian French Marxist, and his followers rejected "ministerialism," that is participation in a bourgeois government. Other socialists took a different stance: Jean Gars (1859–1914) and his supporters viewed the event was unique, although they argued that in general, a socialist should not enter a non-socialist government. Meanwhile, the French syndicalists pointed to the Millerand affair as proof of the corrupting influence of electoral politics.

The Guesdists established the Socialist Party of France, and Jaurès organized the French Socialist Party while the increasingly conservative Millerand continued to refer to himself as a "socialist" for some time to come. At the Amsterdam Congress of the Second International held in 1904, international pressure united the two parties into the French Section of the Workers' International (SFIO), but the divisions remained despite profuse declarations of "revolutionary unity."

The Millerand case was far from exceptional, and everywhere when similar problems arose they strained socialist unity. In Italy, the clever liberal politician Giolitti almost convinced the reformist socialist Filippo Turati (1857–1932) to join his government in 1903. In reality, Turati would have certainly joined Giolitti if it had not been for the fierce opposition of his party, the Italian Socialist Party (PSI). Later in 1912, the PSI was compelled to expel a member who could not be convinced to reject the lure of government office. As rigid and sectarian as this attitude against cooperation in non-socialist governments might sound, there were coherent reasons behind it. Once in office, socialists would be forced by the press of events to take responsibility for the actions of a government they could not control. Moreover, the trappings of power associated with cabinet offices were such that many socialists were seduced into becoming less and less radical. These socialists began to enjoy office so much that they forgot about taking power. Millerand was to turn dramatically to the right over time, for example, ending his career as an opponent of socialism.

The Split in Russian Socialism

Although little noted at the time, the debates over reformism were to reverberate to the eastern part of the European continent, that is, to the Czar's Russia. The socialist movement in Russia was markedly different from that in the rest of Europe, due to the political differences of the czarist nation. One important difference was that there existed no parliament which radicals could hope to conquer. With the exception of the absolute divine right monarchy of Russia, all of Europe's more undemocratic countries had some type of representative body. Furthermore, the repression of dissidents of any sort was of a type that made Bismarck's anti-socialist law seem almost liberal in comparison. These conditions forced Russian socialists to face a far different set of problems than their western European counterparts.

Although Russian socialists did not have to worry about the potentially corrupting influence of cabinet positions, their movement was, nevertheless, to divide over the reform versus revolution debate. Since parliamentarianism was hardly a threat in a nation without a parliament, the rift occurred over the issue of party membership. Formed in 1898, the much persecuted Russian Social Democratic Labor Party (RSDLP) had never amounted to much by western standards. Driven underground by fierce repression and handicapped by the small size of the Russian working class, the RSDLP was far from important within the Second International. Even when they used the same language as western Marxists, the Russians remained peripheral to the mainstream of the socialist movement.

Few observers outside the Czar's realm, therefore, took note of the significance of the 1903 RSDLP Congress which had to be held outside Russia. During the meetings, Lenin was able to narrowly gain a majority for a more disciplined, centralized party organization. This new party was to be made up of professional revolutionaries willing to carry out orders from central directing bodies. The opposition to Lenin had fought to maintain a much more western style party with looser membership requirements. Behind this dispute loomed many other issues. Lenin wanted a strict party discipline largely to prevent reformism, while many of his opponents fought against him precisely in order to allow reformism. This dispute would split Russian socialism into Lenin's supporters, henceforth known as "Bolsheviks" (from the Russian word for majority), and those opposed, now known as "Mensheviks" (minority).

This new, vanguard party which Lenin set about constructing was firmly committed to an insurrectionary road to socialism. Lenin's party was to be a cadre of professional revolutionaries who would seek to be the vanguard of the working class rather than actually win over a majority of the population as most socialists sought to do. It rejected the idea of pushing for liberalization as a step towards socialism as well as "economism" which stressed concentration on labor's struggle for economic improvement. Impatient to follow the steps which revolutionaries had walked in the west, Lenin sought to bypass the stage of liberal democracy and jump to socialism by way of insurrection. Whereas most European radicals like Kautsky (whom Lenin greatly admired up until 1914) wanted to use parliament and democratic rights to make revolutionary changes, the Bolsheviks were committed to revolution, first and foremost. Ironically, Lenin thought that he was simply applying the practice of European social democracy, and especially German socialism, to Russian conditions. In reality, the Mensheviks were in most ways more like the socialist parties of the West.

The split in the Russian party was not given undue consideration elsewhere. After all, almost no one expected a revolution in Russia. Marx (and almost everyone else who had thought about it) had maintained that the revolution would come first in an industrialized nation with a large proletariat, such as Germany. Backward Russia with its almost feudal political system and massive peasantry seemed the least likely place for socialism, since it lacked even the minimum economic preconditions. In all probability, most Russian workers found the differences between the competing socialist groups incomprehensible. Not because they lacked an interest in socialism but more because workers were more concerned with action rather than theoretical debates. The only noticeable difference to the average person was that the Bolsheviks were more efficient and better organized.

Still as one of the few non-Russians to take interest, Rosa Luxemburg, argued that Lenin's Bolshevik party ran the danger of substituting the party for the proletariat. Luxemburg also feared that such a centralized party would stifle the masses and democracy. Later events, particularly once Stalin seized power, would prove her fears well founded. This was not, however, Lenin's intention. He sincerely felt that the only way a socialist party could resist the temptations of reformism was to have a firm party structure. He often likened the Bolsheviks to the German Social Democrats during their years of illegal functioning under the anti-socialist law and looked forward to the day when the red flag flying over Berlin would signal a European-wide insurrection. Further, in the years before 1914, Lenin still considered himself a disciple of Kautsky, who was to become one of Lenin's harshest critics.

Anarchist Alienation from Socialism

Not surprisingly, the anarchists greeted splits within European socialist movement with glee. For the orthodox anarchist, the growth of reformism within the mainstream revolutionary movement was proof that they had been right all along. For the anarchists, Bernstein, Millerand and all the other manifestations of "revisionism" were merely the logical conclusion to socialism's emphasis on electoral politics. While reformists sought to brand their radical socialist opponents as semi-anarchist, European anarchists saw these charges as further evidence that they, not the socialists, were the true revolutionaries.

Unfortunately for the anarchists, they were in no position to capitalize on the difficulties confronting their socialist rivals. In most northern European countries like Germany and Sweden, anarchism flourished among a few cafe intellectuals who lacked any mass influence. Even in nations like Italy and Spain where anarchism could truly be termed a movement, it was to suffer massive setbacks due to its association with "propaganda of the deed." A brief look at events in Spain will illustrate this continuing anarchist dilemma.

Although Spanish anarchists had real roots within sections of the population, they were subject to waves of repression and public repulsion due to the propensity of some of their number to set off bombs. Despite the rejection of terror by many leading anarchists, the cities of Spain were to see numerous explosions set by men who proclaimed themselves anarchists. Most of these bombings were random acts of frustration and typically lacked so much as a clear target. The bombs utilized were crude, homemade instruments which usually caused a minimum of physical damage. Still, they provided the Spanish authorities an excuse to assert that dynamite was, in the words of one anarchist's lament, "synonymous with anarchism."

In April 1892, the Spanish police arrested a Frenchman and his Portuguese collaborator in a plot to blow up the Cortes (parliament). By planning to blow up a symbol of what little democracy there was in the country, these anarchists were hardly endeared to the non-terrorist left. Despite the foreign origins of the would-be bombers, the government used this and numerous other lesser incidents to create a special anti-anarchist police unit known as the Brigada Social. This unit's attempt to destroy underground cells was to prove uniquely ineffective. After all, there really was no central anarchist conspiracy which could be discovered and its members thrown in jail. Most bombings were the work of isolated individuals, small splinter groups, or even, as in the case of the attempted Cortes bombing and the 1897 assassination of the Spanish prime minister by an Italian, foreign anarchists.

Yet, the Brigada Social was to cause much disruption within the ranks of the Spanish left. The Brigada's reliance on criminals and paid informants was of marginal utility in preventing bombings. Yet, these men were not above planting evidence on those the police sought to arrest or throwing a few bombs if the Brigada desired a pretense to engage in a general crackdown. Since the anarchist belief in the "propaganda of the deed" was always a ready excuse to strengthen the state's repressive apparatus, the mutual hostility between socialists and anarchists was certainly magnified. This hatred was inevitable since one might say the former group wished to be elected to parliament while the latter wanted to blow it up.

The cycle of anarchist violence followed by massive governmental repression continued throughout the twentieth century. The immediate loser in this political battle was the anarchist movement which saw its leaders jailed or exiled and all manifestations of public activity severely attacked. Yet in the early twentieth century, a revived anarchist tendency became instrumental in the birth of a powerful syndicalist union—the *Confederación Nacional del Trabajo* (CNT).

Syndicalism's Challenge to Socialism

The Spanish CNT, founded in 1910, was to have a profound impact on the history of that nation particularly during the Civil War of 1936–39. Developing about a decade after the French CGT, the Spanish *Confederación Nacional del Trabajo* enrolled only 15,000 workers as of 1915. During the next few years the syndicalist seed was to grow on Spanish soil. By 1919, the CNT increased to a membership of about 700,000. This massive growth was accomplished in the context of a rapid industrialization which transformed hundreds of thousands of peasants into urban workers. As in France, the anarchist belief in "propaganda of the deed" receded as syndicalist trade unionists promoted adherence to the idea of the general strike.

As with the French CGT, the CNT viewed trade unions struggles as the most meaningful method of class struggle. On a day-to-day basis, the CNT promoted strikes and often industrial sabotage as weapons to improve the condition of their members. Members of the CNT believed that the first step was the establishment of anarcho-syndicalist organizations across Spain. Then when this structure was robust enough to uphold a new society, a general strike would be called which would sweep away the old institutions. The organization believed that if the overwhelming majority of workers failed to report to their place of employment the economy would collapse along with all the bourgeois political structures.

This model of revolution had a certain appeal particularly in a newly industrializing society like Spain. Reformism, which appeared endemic in the Socialist International, was thought not to be a possibility in syndicalist organizations by either by most syndicalists or even their enemies. As events in France would show, this was an illusion. True, the French CGT went on record during its Amiens Congress of 1906 as rejecting all political alliances in favor of complete trade union independence. Rather, the CGT argued, a federation of unions would bring together "all workers who are conscious of the need to struggle for the abolition of the wage system" and not concern themselves with electoral politics or parties. But the most solemn proclamations cannot preclude political pressures in the real world.

Although formed by an anarchist, the *Confédération Générale du Travail* was never of one mind when it came to political ideology. In addition to anarchists, there were "pure" syndicalists and socialists in the ranks of the CGT. There existed a minority reformist current within the organization which wished to avoid not only political affiliations but wanted to concentrate solely on economic activities. Although the revolutionaries had a clear majority, this minority was by no means insignificant. Reformism was so strong in the last years of the nineteenth century that the leaders of the CGT's left wing saw "domestication" or taming of the workers movement a greater danger than outright repression. For the time being, the revolutionaries within the trade unions maintained the upper hand.

The fears of the radicals were not unfounded given that this was precisely what reformist socialists set out to do. By a combination of social reforms and economic concessions, many reformists, particularly Millerand, hoped that militant unionism would be supplanted by a social partnership between the government and the workers where cooperation would replace conflict. Not wishing to tie their working class members to capitalism, the bulk of the CGT firmly resisted these appeals. Refusing to comply with governmental policies which they felt would turn the trade unions into agencies for disciplining labor, the CGT provoked not only strong government reaction, but also the consolidation of the employers' organizations.

In itself, this was a familiar story and one would expect little else from the government in the face of a self-avowed revolutionary union movement. After 1900, the ministers responsible for the squashing of militant worker's actions were either socialists or ex-socialists. After Millerand, there was René Viviani who assumed the post of Minister of Labor in the 1906 government of Georges Clemenceau (1841–1929). More scandalous for revolutionaries, however, were the actions of Aristide Briand (1862–1932). Briand had been associated with the extreme left and had even been an outspoken advocate of the general strike. Suddenly changing his political philosophy, he joined the Clemenceau government in 1906 and was expelled from the Socialist Party. In 1910, as Prime Minister, he shattered the railroad strike by holding stations with army troops. Further, Briand called up railroad workers who were army reservists and compelled them to break their own strike.

Thus, the action of certain socialists confirmed in the minds of many CGT members the folly of hoping for change through the political process. This alienation from politics was increased by the legal status of trade unions. The Act of 1884 which gave workers the right of association did not apply to government workers. While informal associations of public employees were tolerated, the government reserved the right to dissolve as unlawful any group which sought to act like a trade union. As the CGT organizing efforts began to make headway among elementary school teachers and postal workers, a conflict became inevitable.

In March 1909, French postal workers went out on strike in hopes of removing the generally detested Minister who presided over them. Taken unprepared, the Clemenceau government convinced the postal workers to call off the strike on the strength of a number of implied promises. When the unpopular head of the post office stayed in his position while other promises remained unfulfilled, the workers resumed their work stoppage. This second strike was less solid and the CGT's attempts to gain support from other unions gained little response. Seeing the postal worker's weakness, the government crushed their organization by mass firings of the most militant union members. The CGT was helpless in the face of this governmental onslaught. This defeat created a deep sense of bitterness and betrayal within the CGT who saw politicians, now more than ever, as a plague to be hated and avoided. Of course, the ruthless suppression of the railroad workers the following year was to further convince the *Confédération Générale du Travail* of the merits of anti-parliamentarianism.

European Radicalism: The View from Below

So far, prominent individuals or mighty (and not so mighty) organizations and the profound social forces which gave rise to them have been discussed. What, however, did the average European worker make of all these political events, proclamations and infighting? In this realm, official political pronouncements, theoretical tomes or the speeches of famous revolutionaries are of little value. Since there existed few of the modern techniques for discovering public opinion, any investigation into the attitudes of the ordinary European must remain speculative. That having been said, and understanding there is no clear-cut way of accessing the mind-set of millions of long dead individuals, we can look at evidence which suggests how the common people reacted to European radicalism.

Firstly, information can be gleaned from election results from those nations which had more or less free elections (this excludes Czarist Russia, of course). In addition, since membership figures exist for the various organizations associated with the revolutionary movement, these numbers suggest a certain minimum base of support. Finally, there does exist some first hand data in the form of diaries, memoirs and police spy reports which help round out the overall picture of everyday perceptions. Looking at vote totals, it would seem that the left grew stronger with each passing generation well into the twentieth century. This is not only true for the well known case of Germany where the Social Democrats were the single largest party by World War I, but also for other nations as well. In the Kingdom of Sweden, to cite only one example, the Social Democratic Labor Party (SDLP) garnered 28.5% of the votes cast in the 1911 balloting, a percentage that rose to 36.4% by 1914. Sweden, which was the scene of alternately bitter strikes and lock outs up until the 1930s, was home to a mere 3,194 SDLP members in 1889, the year the Second International was established. By 1914, this puny number had grown to 84,410 dues paying party members in a country of under six million inhabitants.

Similar numbers could be provided throughout western Europe to show that the official socialist movement had wide support in terms of both voter support and membership participation. Of course, the movement was stronger in some areas (particularly in the more industrialized nations) than others and support vacillated from year to year. All in all, however, the trend was clearly upward. Likewise, trade unions, considered an integral part of the movement, enjoyed a momentous surge in membership. By 1912, there were 1,064,000 trade unionists in France and 2,553,000 union members in Germany. Meanwhile, the trend setter in labor organizing, Great Britain, had 4,135,000 organized workers by 1913.

Still, the objection could quite rightly be raised that these statistics prove nothing about the actual consciousness of the average person. After all, no doubt many socialist voters and trade union members were more motivated by the desire for reforms than belief in revolution. So, to attempt to delve more deeply into the actual thoughts of these individuals, it is necessary to examine evidence other than these statistics.

A careful study of proletarian attitudes indicates that workers were neither the stereotypical revolutionary machines betrayed by corrupt leaders nor the vile racist and sexist creatures of bourgeois caricature. The true picture of workers is clearly far more complex than the one dimensional views often put forth. Most workers who identified with socialism appear to have considered themselves people of science who rejected religion. That is, they saw the revolution as unfolding according to what they held to be the laws of historical development. Thus, they saw little contradiction between reforms today and revolution tomorrow. Belief in revolution gave them dignity and the promise of a better life. Most importantly, all the available reports from government agents and worker's diaries indicate that it was their hard everyday life with its miserable economic conditions which made revolution appear, to them, not only desirable but inescapable.

Naturally, sentiments among workers were volatile and people would change their mind from one day to the next, as is true today. In one context, a worker would embrace revolution while in another circumstance the same individual would support reform. Yet then, as now, most people's attitudes were conditional not absolute. Although there was prejudice, racism and bigotry among members of the left, what is truly astounding is how little there actually was. Being oppressed themselves, most workers tended to sympathize with the "under dogs" whether they were colonial subjects or oppressed national minorities.

A brief look at some of these sources should illustrate these points. After his father died and his mother developed cancer, one British worker who spent his early years in workhouses, commented that "my childhood's experience made me feel more bitter against the present system, and more earnest in my efforts towards changing it." The theme of the inhumanity of capitalism turns up frequently among radicalized workers. The embittered worker often saw revolution as the only possible means to a "level the playing field." One German miner when asked what his fondest dream was responded: "My foremost wish is to carry the banner when the war against the capitalists and Junker comes and to mow them down to the last man." Such intense bitterness may not be typical, yet it represented a clear point of view among more radical workers.

German police reports on conversations held in proletarian taverns in Hamburg show how many workers responded to the revisionist controversy. Most seem to have rejected Bernstein and his revision of Marxism. This disapproval appears to be based not on hostility to new ideas, but because reformist theory did not correspond to their everyday reality. Huddled over beer after a hard day of labor, these workers thought that the revisionists were "from the bourgeois camp" who wished to destroy Social Democracy as a worker's party. Feelings such as these are not particularly strange, for the progressive changes that Bernstein had suggested were occurring in capitalism made only a slight difference for the average worker. Harassed by police, bullied at work and often short of money, the proletarian radical was far less likely to see compromise or coopera-tion as viable strategies.

Of course, all workers were far from revolutionary even in the most radical of times. The story of how one socialist woman at-tempted to convert her traditionally minded mother illustrates this reality. In her autobiography, Adelheid Popp describes the objections her widowed mother raised to her involvement with the socialist movement. Particularly distressing to the elder Popp was her daugh-ter's rejection of religion. Thinking that her long suffering mother rejected her logical arguments in favor of socialism because they came from her child, Adelheid was thrilled when Frederick Engels and August Bebel agreed to visit her home. After an evening of explaining to the mother why she should be proud of her daughter, these two famous socialists left. When mother and daughter were alone, Adel-heid was asked "why do you bring old men here?" Ironically, Popp's mother had neglected the thrust of the discussion and instead focused on the unsuitability of either man as a potential husband for her daughter.

In the end, many workers, like Popp's mother, were too bound up in older traditions of religion and family to consider the socialist movement of interest. Perhaps the best way to view the outlook of common people towards social revolution is to emphasize its con-stantly evolving nature. Often, the once conservative peasant quickly became radicalized when forced by economic change to become an urban worker. The revolutionary often looked more to immediate reforms during periods of improvement in the standard of living. Workers could demonstrate for peace one week and support war as self defense the next. As the revolutionary Rosa Luxemburg remarked, the masses were like the sea: calm and peaceful one moment, rough and stormy the next. The ebbs and flows of the revolutionary move-ment in the next decades would confirm this standpoint.

The European Left at the End of the 19th Century

For all the apparent unity publicly proclaimed (at least among members of the socialist camp) the European left entered the twentieth century deeply divided. The split was not merely between anarchists and syndicalists on the one side and adherents of the Second International on the other. In addition to all the inevitable personal disputes and cliques which accompany any large movement, there emerged three shifting and ill-defined, yet nonetheless distinctive, tendencies within the nominally revolutionary movement. Although one could divide and subdivide these into dozens of conflicting currents, these trends may be grouped into three general ideological affinities.

First, there were those who could no longer be considered revolutionary even in the broadest sense of the word. Within the Socialist International, this would include people like Bernstein and his fellow revisionists. In addition, there were many so-called syndicalists or even anarchists who had long ago despaired of revolution and saw their activity as a means to pressure for economic concessions or political reforms. From the reformists in the CGT to the "practical" members of British labor, these individuals seemed radical only from the biased view of the reactionary press.

Next, there was the largest single tendency within the left, which might be termed the center group, its members believed in a revolutionary transformation of society, albeit by working through existing institutions. These people believed that the world of equality they sought would be achieved by pushing forward ever stronger radical institutions. For syndicalists and other trade unionists, this suggested that a powerful labor organization would one day render the capitalists passé and power would pass quickly into the hands of the proletariat. For socialists, this denoted traveling the "parliamentary road to socialism" which meant laboring for the day when an elected majority could legislate revolutionary social change.

Finally, there was a minority of resolute revolutionaries who rejected both compromise with capitalism and condemned "parliamentary cretinism" as a strategy for failure. While agreeing on the necessity of fighting for immediate reforms, these people looked to the example of the Paris Commune and argued that the existing structures of society had to be replaced entirely. For anarchists, this meant an end to all governmental apparatus while for revolutionary socialists it meant the creation of a new worker's state. That these differences were of more than academic interest would be shown by the dramatic events in years to come.

4. The Left Confronts Militarism, Colonialism and Rebellion

As industrial capitalism destroyed the traditional community—be it village or parish—people experienced a void in their lives which many did not fill with the internationalist sentiment of the left. Particularly among the hard pressed peasantry and the alienated middle class, this emotional vacuum was frequently filled with the nostalgic faith in their respective nation. Furthermore, xenophobia and anti-Semitism became alluring emotions for many battered by the forces of modernization in the later part of the nineteenth century.

As nationalism, anti-Semitism and rightist ideologies grew in strength, the left was to be forced to fight not only the established elites but movements of the radical right—thinking these movements were born out of ignorance, the revolutionary left tended to underestimate their potential appeal; believing that attitudes like anti-Semitism were antiqued remnants from a less enlightened past. With the advance of science and the spread of education, irrational ideologies of the right were expected to wither and eventually, disappear leading the formerly deluded supporters of the right into the left's camp. After all, "Anti-Semitism," as August Bebel had commented, "is the socialism of fools." Once these "fools" wised up, they would naturally reject the counterfeit ideas of racism and embrace the genuine article of socialism.

As it turned out, this prediction was far wide of the mark. The history of the twentieth century has illustrated the staying power of nationalism and indeed racism. While the left had some notable degree of success in preventing these ideologies from infecting members of their movement, they seriously underestimated the appeal of "nation" and "blood" among many Europeans. Thus, revolutionaries entered the twentieth century woefully unprepared to combat what would prove to be their greatest challenges. The problems they encountered when faced with growing militarism, swelling arms budgets and the threat of war illustrate their predicament.

Militarism and the Threat of War

European radicalism was, in many ways, the child of the Enlightenment of the eighteenth century. As such, it had inherited the ideals of world peace and internationalism. Socialists looked towards the day when the world was one unified federal social republic consisting of all nations. This republic would eliminate national conflicts and eradicate war forever. Anarchists and syndicalists, while rejecting even such a benign form of government, also looked forward to a world of peace.

Radicals of almost all ideologies agreed that war inherently grew out of the barbarism of the existing order. As an inevitable instrument of foreign policy, war was part of the struggle of competing ruling classes to enlarge their sphere of economic and political power. For the victorious rulers, it brought added wealth and authority. For the average citizen, war promised only death and taxes. Revolutionaries viewed the fight to prevent war as an integral part of the struggle to destroy a social system which promoted violence. That the peoples of the world should unite to avert war was agreed upon easily, how to accomplish this was not.

One aspect of this struggle was the question of standing, that is to say professional, armies. This type of army, which was typical in most of Europe except Switzerland, was considered a machine designed for conquest, if not a major cause of warfare itself. At the founding congress of the Second International in 1889, standing armies were declared to be "incompatible with any democratic and republican regime." The professional army, with its officer corps drawn from the upper crust of society, was condemned as not only an enemy of peace, but also antagonistic to democracy since it was habitually an "instrument of reactionary coup d'état and social repression." Therefore, the Socialist International called for the replacement of the standing army with the "people in arms."

This idea of a popular militia was thought to satisfy the need for national self-defense while at the same time preventing the military from being used for either internal repression or external adventure. By instituting a system of universal military service where the army would, in effect, be composed of the citizens of the country, as in Switzerland, socialists hoped that the urge towards aggression could be blunted. Yet socialists knew that if such a system could be forced upon an unwilling ruling class, which would be difficult, this would only preclude openly aggressive acts of conquest not wars dressed up in the costume of self defense.

Of greater difficulty was the more fundamental conflict which existed for those who believed capitalism was the root cause of warfare. If wars were an inherent part of capitalist society, as almost all radicals believed, how could such carnage be avoided until that day when the system was overthrown? One possible solution to this predicament was to prepare workers to respond to any outbreak of hostilities by launching a general strike. This idea was undeniably the most prevalent attitude among anarchists and syndicalists. Only after the Belgian general strike for suffrage expansion and the 1905 revolt in Russia would the mainstream radical movement seriously consider this idea. Still within the Socialist International, there was some support for this perspective as shown by the motion introduced by Dutch delegation which submitted a resolution calling upon affiliated parties to "respond to any declaration of war with an appeal to the people for a general cessation of work."

This motion failed to pass because most delegates feared committing themselves to a course of action which they lacked the numbers to actualize. Some socialists, like Plekhanov of Russia, even expressed qualms about asking reservists to resist being called into the army. After all, he argued, this would mean the nations with the strongest socialist movements would be disarmed in the face of countries like Russia, where the movement was weakest. Instead, the International agreed "to protest, ceaselessly and powerfully against the will to war in all its forms, and those alliances which inevitably give rise to war" while urging socialists in legislative bodies "to vote against military credits, to denounce militarism and to advocate disarmament."

Despite these brave words and the repeated discussions on the danger of war within socialist parties and the Socialist International, the outlook of most socialists was one of resignation. They failed to see how they could actually prevent their governments from embarking on wars, short of social revolution itself. If revolution was not yet plausible, then all one could do was wait. Some day they hoped to eliminate capitalism and with it the threat of war. For the moment, they could only protest the possibility of war and affirm their commitment to peace.

One less passive response to the danger of war was the growth of radical anti-militarist propaganda. Particularly in France and later in Germany, Italy and Belgium, there developed a movement to educate workers, particularly young workers, about the evils of militarism. Karl Liebknecht (1871–1919), son of SPD founder Wilhelm, was particularly active in this movement. However, even the younger Liebknecht who was later to help found the German Communist Party tried to keep his anti-militaristic endeavors within the letter of the law. (He wound up spending time in jail for his activities all the same). In their desire to avoid a premature confrontation with powerful governments, most European socialists fell into a deep fatalism.

Still, most revolutionaries did not think war was necessarily inevitable. Some felt that capitalism could be pulled back from the brink of war by vigorous mass protests. Others, like Karl Kautsky, argued that capitalism had become so interconnected across borders of nation-states that the capitalists themselves would refrain from a European-wide conflict since it would be pointless for one branch of a company to blow up another. France's Jean Jaurès held out hope for a general strike or mass uprising which would cause the wheels of war to grind to a halt. Within the socialist world, however, most agreed with August Bebel, when he said, at the 1907 Stuttgart congress of the International, "We can do nothing but patiently explain, open men's minds, agitate and organize."

Although the socialists had no ready solution to the problem of war, the anarchists and syndicalists were worse off. At least the Second International possessed a clear program for a democratized military, anti-militarist education, and public agitation against military expenditures. Many anarchists and syndicalists, however, thought that a major war would be greeted by a spontaneous general strike. Reasoning that war would bring only misery to the mass of Europe's population, they believed that antiwar sentiment would be overwhelming. They believed that the majority of common people would reject the seductive promise of nationalism and firmly resist participating in any future militarist-sponsored bloodshed. Repeatedly, they issued stirring declarations warning the rulers that any attempt at war would be answered by mass insurrection.

In spite of bold proclamations, their strategy was the same as the socialists. That is, to agitate, educate, and organize against capitalism (which caused wars) in order to prepare for the general strike. The key difference between the anarchist groups and the majority of socialists was that the latter were far more realistic about the difficulties in rousing the masses at the outbreak of a war. If World War I was to find the socialists' words about peace abandoned because most supported their governments, the situation was not much better for anarchists who bitterly watched one of their most renown theorists, Peter Kropotkin (1842–1921), publicly endorse the allies' war against the Kaiser's Germany.

Although they might have resisted the comparison, European revolutionaries found themselves in very much the same position as the Christian churches. Both the Christian churches and the European left proclaimed the evils of war and the universal nature of their ideas. And most radicals, like the majority of their Christian counterparts, would wind up supporting their national governments in time of war. Before the First World War, many churchmen felt it unthinkable that Christian would slay Christian. On the left, that worker would slay worker was equally unthinkable to radicals. In both cases, the unthinkable became not only thought but deed.

Encountering the Problem of Colonialism

The roughly forty years before the start of World War I in 1914 was noted not only for the spread of militarism and the growing menace of war. It was also the "Age of Empire" when the major European powers (and to a lesser extent the United States and Japan) divided up immense territories inhabited by less militarily advanced peoples. Within a historically short period of time after the 1870s, the world was divided into the rich and powerful (mainly European nations) and the poor and weak (primarily African, Asian or Latin American nations).

Approximately a quarter of the earth's land fell to the onslaught of a handful of dominant nations while the formerly independent inhabitants were reduced to the status of colonial subjects with few rights. In the period from 1876 to 1915, Great Britain alone amassed 4,000,000 square miles of new territories with France coming in a close second with 3,500,000. Even tiny Belgium and relatively weak Italy were able to carve out immense empires of slightly under a million square miles each. Germany, only unified in 1871 and a relative late comer to the scramble for colonies, was still forceful enough to conquer a land mass of over 1,000,000 square miles.

Quite aside from the brutal nature of colonial rule, colonialism was part of the process of creating a single global economy. In fact, no one at the time would have questioned the underlying economic basis for Europe's charge into other parts of the globe. Further, the conspicuous fact was that the peoples conquered were of a different race than Europeans. It was a comfortable notion to imply the fairer skinned Europeans had some sort of right (if not duty) to control peoples with dark skins who lived in areas remote from "civilized" Europe. The rulers of Europe found it quite convenient to suggest that "white Christians" should band together in order to convert the "dark heathens." In a word, among the powerful, there were those who sought to replace class consciousness with racial awareness. Consequently, the creation of colonial empires would be of great concern for the European left.

At least as far back as the creation of the First International, revolutionaries had explicitly affirmed the principle of the basic equality of all races. All the world's peoples were seen as having the rights to freedom and national independence. Moreover, the belief in international solidarity among all oppressed peoples was a bedrock of revolutionary doctrine for most leftists. For example, Marx had singled out the solidarity of British workers with the North during the Civil War for particular praise arguing "labor in a white skin can never be free when labor in a black skin is enslaved." As mentioned previously, one of the first actions the General Council of the IWMA undertook was to send an address of congratulations to U.S. President Abraham Lincoln (1809–1865) in support of his war against slavery.

Nor did the average worker show much interest in backing colonial adventure. There is little evidence that the European lower classes showed much enthusiasm for colonialism, in general, and even less for the wars which inevitably accompanied imperial conquests. In the case of British opposition to the Boer War, there was substantial peril that the left would find itself temporarily isolated in the climate of jingoism which the conflict set off. Yet, the left seldom wavered in its resistance. In actuality, the revolutionaries stuck to their internationalist principles more than could have been expected given the white heat of nationalism which burned at the moment. Of course, revisionists or reformists, like England's Sidney Webb (1859–1947), Italy's Turati, or Germany's Bernstein, discovered reasons to promote their nation's colonial ambitions. However, any other attitude would have been inconsistent as these reformists stressed the advantages that colonialism gave to indigenous peoples in the form of economic development.

Aside from reformists, the majority of the left was firmly anti-colonial for both moral and practical reasons. It was radicals, including American author Mark Twain (1835–1910), who revealed to the world the appalling barbarism of Belgian colonial rule in the Congo (where mine owners would cut off hands of African workers as punishment for insubordination). This anti-colonial stance was often unpopular particularly among the middle class elements upon whom many socialists depended upon for electoral support. For instance, in 1907, the German SPD refused to support its nation's expansion into South-West Africa. During the elections which followed, the socialists were punished by middle class swing voters for this stance, and the party suffered its largest electoral setback of that time.

In southern Europe, militant members of the Italian Socialist Party (PSI) spearheaded the fight against the Libyan war of 1911, which cost the party support and landed many radicals in jail. Nor was the reaction of the Italian left to this colonial escapade merely rhetorical. Not content with only speeches or leaflets, many leftists—socialist, anarchists or syndicalist—took more militant action. On September 28, 1911, a twenty-four-hour general strike against the war revealed the anti-colonial attitude of many workers particularly in the so-called red belt of northern Italy. In addition to strikes, there were assorted direct actions, including attempts to sabotage the movement of troops by pulling up railroad rails and fire bombing railway stations.

Yet, these same anti-colonial radicals did almost nothing to help organize the resistance of colonial subjects to their rulers. With few exceptions, little was actually done to facilitate the anti-colonial movements by European socialists until the creation of the Communist International. There were Dutch revolutionaries who aided the peoples of Indonesia, but that was markedly the exception, not the rule. Once again, the left saw colonialism as an outgrowth of capitalism. And once again, most leftists believed that there was little that could be done until capitalism was overthrown, save to protest and to "open men's minds." Moreover, leftists had little contact with non-Europeans and were apt to be condescending towards "less developed" peoples. This sometimes took the form of viewing colonial people as primarily a source of cheap labor and, hence, a threat to organized European labor. At other times, pressure from the nationalistic press, military, and government caused socialists and other radicals to avoid the issue of colonialism in favor of discussing domestic problems. Given their contradictory feelings about colonial peoples, it is not a surprise that the manner in which prominent radicals responded to colonial issues was not always the most principled.

For instance, in one hotly contested election campaign, Philipp Scheidemann (1865–1939), a German Social Democrat was assailed by his bourgeois opponent for his party's opposition to colonialism. During a debate, the socialist was challenged to explain how he could oppose the expansion of German colonies in Africa when his constituents would benefit from increased export of locally produced metal products such as knifes. Reluctant to open up a discussion of the morality of colonialism, the SPD candidate responded with a cheap retort. Why would Africans buy German knives, asked the socialist candidate, since they do not wear pants and have no pockets to put knives in? Although he won the Reichstag seat, this type of response did little to deepen the understanding of the average citizen concerning overseas imperial policy.

The Case of the Boer War

What was the response of the average worker to colonial adventure? Were they swept away with patriotic fever as has so often been suggested? An examination of the response of the British proletariat to the second Boer war may be indicative of working class attitudes towards imperial wars of conquest. Unlike other victims of colonialism who were dark skinned, the Boers were the descendants of Dutch settlers in Southern Africa. When huge gold deposits were discovered in the Transvaal region in the late 1880s, the British moved steadily into Boer territory. The attempts of the Boer government to preserve its independence infuriated English colonialists like Cecil Rhodes (1853–1902).

After a series of provocations on both sides, war broke out in October 1899. The 60,000 men the Boers were able to put into the field faced 350,000 British soldiers until the Empire's victory in 1902. The spectacle of the vastly outnumbered Boers fighting almost six times their number and the widely held belief that the war was about little else besides gold did nothing to promote the good name of the British Empire. Within Great Britain, however, the war was the occasion for a hysterical wave of pro-imperialist sentiment. Typically racism is thought of as being directed against members of a different racial group, particularly the prejudice of whites against peoples of color. The Boer War proved that this need not be the case.

Although the Boers were white, the British popular press was full of the most vile racist slanders. The Boers were explicitly portrayed as being on a lower rung on the evolutionary ladder than British people. In numerous articles and stories, the Boers were painted as a savage and uncivilized "race" that was filthy, dishonest, degenerate and devious. The creator of Sherlock Holmes, Sir Arthur Conan Doyle (1859–1930) joined in this campaign of libel in 1900 with his *The Great Boer War*. In this work, he characterized the Boers as "simple primitive men" who failed to understand the ways of civilization. This primitive existence resulted from, in Conan Doyle's words, the semitropical sun "waking strange ferments" in the blood. (Of course the Boers were not the only targets of the author's prejudices, "hideous aborigines" were dismissed as the "lowest of the human race" while even the British army was advised to draw recruits from a higher class since "modern warfare demands more intelligence" than was to be found in the peasant or laborer classes). Combined with this printed evidence, historians have pointed to the mass excitement caused by war news as proof that the war had popular support. In Great Britain, large and disorderly crowds often damaged property of suspected "pro-Boers."

Moreover, there was a general election held in 1900 known to history as the "Khaki Election" because of the centrality of the war issue. This balloting resulted in a Conservative (or Tory) Party landslide as the pro-war government was returned with a 134-seat majority. Such results would seem to further bolster the claim that the average Briton supported the government's colonial war. On closer examination, matters turn out to be much less clear cut.

The existence of sizeable pro-war sentiment in Great Britain at the time cannot be disputed. On that the evidence is clear. The question is, however, was this attitude predominant among the left's constituency, the working class? More than just the volume of anti-Boer racism in print which, after all, did not emanate from the proletariat, the tumultuous pro-war crowds and the 1900 election results would appear to indicate widespread support even among British labor. A closer investigation of the available evidence, however, leads to quite a different conclusion.

Working class institutions, such as the London Trades Council, accused the government of using the war as a means to divert attention from pressing social problems. In contrast to the mainstream press, numerous labor and left periodicals, like *Club Life* and *ILP News*, attacked the war as avoidable and a drain on resources needed for social services like public hospitals. The crowds which disrupted peace rallies turned out to be other than working class in composition. The evidence indicates that the vast majority of anti-Boer demonstrations were the work of overly excited young middle-class patriots. As one laborer remarked, after a pro-war mob surged through Trafalgar Square, he found it strange the "respectable classes" turned out to be the ones in favor of rowdyism.

Even the "Khaki Election" of 1900 fails to establish the view that the working masses were pro-war. A careful analysis of the election returns in predominantly working class districts, many of which would later become Labour Party strongholds, show little pro-war feeling or pro-colonial sympathy. Where Conservative members were returned to parliament, it was because of other local issues, not questions of foreign policy. In those districts where the Conservatives campaigned primarily on the question of support for the Boer War, they were often defeated by Liberal candidates who stressed social issues. For instance, in the traditionally Conservative constituency of Stockport, the Tory candidate who had spent thirteen years in South Africa went down to defeat in face of a Liberal assault on the government's record on social reform.

Thus, it would seem that even the glitter of gold could not convince the bulk of labor to support an imperial foreign policy. Appeals to national pride, racism and promise of increased wealth which would trickle down to the masses were unable to distract workers from the more pressing problems of their everyday lives. So if radical leaders opposed colonialism out of principle, the working class found imperialism at the very least irrelevant to their social and economic predicaments. Their cynicism about the motives behind colonialism, whether accurate or not, prevented most workers from signing onto the campaign of imperialist hysteria.

The Socialist International and Colonialism

As with other issues such as militarism, the socialist parties were in a contradictory position regarding colonialism. This was revealed during the debate on the "colonial question" at the 1907 Stuttgart Congress of the Socialist International. While the majority of delegates repudiated colonialism on principle, for as Kautsky noted, a "socialist colonialism" was impossible, there was, nonetheless, some sentiment which viewed imperialism as part of an inevitable process. This process was linking together the world's economies and peoples and further developing the productive powers of humanity. Thus, in spite of the inhuman administration of the colonies, colonialism was part of an historical process which would ultimately elevate the culture and well being of all people.

The odious nature of colonialism was conceded by all but debate centered around whether it was ultimately a step forward or not. The colonial areas, some socialists argued, would have to pass through a capitalist stage of development before they had the necessary level of development to achieve socialism. Others delegates added that even the most brutal capitalist colonial policy would be develop the productive forces of the colonial territories. These arguments were countered by anti-colonialists who asserted that even the most benevolent colonialism rested ultimately on force and violence.

However, all sides shared serious doubts about the wisdom or even the ability of "colonial" people to govern themselves. This paternalistic attitude would continue until well after World War I with socialists worrying that colonial subjects had to be "educated" for self rule. Moreover, as with the threat of war, the International was powerless to actually influence events before socialism was achieved. Colonialism was seen as inevitable under capitalism, so there was little that could be done but to fight for reforms and try to protect what few rights colonial subjects had.

Despite what may be seen today as the implicit racism in such attitudes, the Socialist International did resolve to castigate colonialism although its members offered little, if any, assistance to the colonial victims. Still the Congress concluded, "capitalist colonial policies must, by their nature, give rise to servitude, forced labor and the extermination of the native peoples in colonized territories." In the unanimously endorsed resolution, the International condemned the "barbarous methods of capitalist colonialism and demands, in the interests of the development of the productive forces, a policy based on peaceful cultural development and one which develops the world's mineral resources in the interests of the whole of humanity." When put in the context of the all prevailing nationalism and even racism of the era, these were indeed brave words. Words, however, that the European left was unable (if not, at times, unwilling) to convert into deeds.

Russia's Revolutionary Dress Rehearsal of 1905

While the major European revolutionary tendencies of all ideologies argued points of theory, an actual revolutionary uprising broke out in the farthest reaches of the European world—Imperial Russia. Throughout Europe and all her social classes by the start of the twentieth century, there existed a feeling that something would have to happen in the land of the Czars. Considered by the rest of Europe as a throwback to feudal times, Russia was an immense, plodding, grossly incompetent, economically and technologically underdeveloped realm.

The Russian empire had 126 million inhabitants by 1897 of whom four out of five were still peasants ruled by a hereditary nobility of only about 1 percent of the population. Although the serfs had finally been freed in 1861, Czarist agriculture remained primitive. For example, by the start of the twentieth century, peasants in the European portion of Russia produced on average only nine bushels of grain per acre compared with the British average of over thirty-five. The Czar ruled his domain through a bureaucratized autocracy, which alternatively ignored then repressed the populace.

The Czarist regime dimly realized the need for modernization around the middle of the nineteenth century and began a weak industrialization campaign in the 1890s. For the average Russian, who continued to farm the land, the industrialization process resulted in high taxes and the diverting of resources from countryside. Massive capital investments, both private and public, resulted in dramatic industrial advances. Between 1890 and 1904, the total railroad mileage of Russia doubled. In addition, the national production of coal, iron, and steel doubled during the last five years of the nineteenth century. For Czarism, an unfortunate byproduct of this economic growth was the creation of a modern working class heavily concentrated in a few major industrial areas in atypically large plants. These workers would, like most other sectors of the population at one time or another, demonstrate incurable hostility toward the government and dedicate themselves to social revolution.

Aware that social unrest and political dissent were on the rise, the Czarist government often found anti-Semitism a handy diversion, which had widespread popular support, unlike the government itself. For instance, in April 1903, several hundred Jews were slaughtered during a pogrom, as anti-Jewish riots were called, which went on for three days. Later an official probe into the events uncovered the fact that the pogrom had the support of the minister for internal affairs. In addition, the Russian Orthodox Church was openly—if not proudly—anti-Semitic. One longtime head of this religious institution remarked that the "Jewish problem" would only be solved when a third of Russia's Jews were converted to Christianity, a third left the country and the remaining third "disappeared." It is not startling, therefore, that Russia's Jewish population became more and more receptive to the appeals of revolutionary movements.

In fact, there was hardly any sector of the population who wasn't potentially interested in some sort of revolution. Due to the completely undemocratic nature of the Czarist government, revolution appeared to be the only road open to anyone who wished for a measure of change. Most of the time, however, average Russian citizens were more concerned with their daily problems and tended to blame their miseries on more minor, and more accessible, tyrants. Given the ignorance and destitution of the Russian masses, it was not therefore surprising that many looked to vodka rather than revolution to sooth their pain. Furthermore, the masses could often be easily convinced that their sorrows were the fault of their Jewish fellow citizens. This was the paradox of Czarist Russian society: that the populace could silently suffer under an oppressive system unthinkable in western Europe for such long periods, and yet it was commonly known that Russian society would one day explode into revolution.

The eruption resulted from Russia's failed imperial expansion in the Far East. Blocked by the more modern states to the west, czarist Russia turned eastward where it quickly ran into the rival expansionism of "tiny" Japan. Overconfident, if not smug in its power, the Russian Empire declared war on Japan in February 1904. Czar Nicholas II (1868–1918), his generals and many thought that Japan would prove not match for the massive Russian bear. The opposite happened and Russia was quickly chastened by its Asian adversaries. This rapid defeat of "mighty" Russia sent shock waves throughout the empire when the fundamental weakness of czarism was revealed.

By 1905, the initial enthusiasm for the war had evaporated, and workers became restless as wages began to fall in part due to the economic dislocation caused by the fighting. The incompetence and corruption of the officer corps increasingly alienated the solders and sailors while the peasants grew more uneasy. Soon strikes broke out in St. Petersburg and Moscow, wide-scale revolt erupted among the peasantry, while the military machine, upon which czarism ultimately depended for survival, began to crumble.

On Sunday, January 9, striking workers and their families peacefully marched to the Czar's winter palace to present a petition in which they humbly asked for reforms. The government's response was as dramatic as it would prove to be counterproductive: troops opened fire on the unarmed crowd hitting thousands. This militaristic act set off a great strike wave which engulfed Russia until late March.

Among the peasantry, who made up the bulk of the population, all the repressed animosity of centuries of oppression burst forth in an orgy of revolt. Momentarily helpless, the nobility watched as 2,000 estates were set aflame. Sailors mutinied at Kronstadt, the naval fortress near St. Petersburg, and within the Black Sea fleet. The mutiny onboard the battleship *Potemkin* was a particularly dramatic affair immortalized by Eisenstein in the later movie of the same name. During the last six months of the year, the military reported eighty-nine outbreaks within its ranks.

Even the end of the catastrophic war with Japan in August had not been sufficient to end the rebellion which would last until almost Christmas. During 1905, which has been called the "dress rehearsal" for the revolution, which would sweep away Czarism twelve years later, two remarkable developments occurred: the mass strike and the formation of workers councils.

Birth of the Soviets

In late 1905, the Russian workers began to form worker's councils which were known by the Russian word *soviets*. These representative bodies, democratically elected by workers, were a new form of mass political power. Leon Trotsky, elected leader of the St. Petersburg soviet, contended that councils were to political action what trade unions were to economic action. Soviets were not the invention of some revolutionary theorist; they developed out of the strike wave which hit Russia in the autumn of 1905.

When on September 19, Moscow typesetters struck over low piece rate payments, the strike quickly spread throughout the city. Then on October 2, the St. Petersburg print workers left work in support of their Moscow counterparts. Five days later, railroad workers began to walk off the job. Soon transportation in much of Russia ground to a halt while more and more factories went on strike. General strikes were called in most important urban areas.

On October 13, the first meeting of the St. Petersburg soviet was called. Each work place was to elect a representative to this central worker's institution although only forty-three people attended the first meeting. Yet as more strikes broke out, more factories sent delegates, with metal workers and print workers quickly joining, followed closely by electric power and textile workers. The soviet movement grew with amazing speed, and less than a month after its birth the St. Petersburg council had 562 members representing about 200,000 workers.

More inclusive than a political party and concerned with issues beyond the normal scope of a trade union, the soviet steadily became a kind of shadow government. The central demands of the workers became more directly political: universal suffrage to an assembly, an end to all censorship, and legalization of workers organizations. The St. Petersburg soviet began to produce its own paper, *Izvestia*, which presented a decidedly different slant on daily events than the mainstream, censored press. Increasingly, average citizens approached the soviet on subjects ranging from appeals for support of wage demands to questions about whether a railroad strike would interrupt a planned trip. When anti-Semites threatened to start pogroms, the soviet organized worker's self-defense squads to patrol the streets. For a period of time in fall 1905, the soviet was in effect the local authority replacing the city government and, at times, even the police. The mass support for the soviet was such that it was able to function unmolested because the government didn't dare attack until it was sure that the danger of successful insurrection had passed.

To counter this spreading revolution, the Czar promised democracy and a constitution on October 16. Although the militant workers of St. Petersburg rejected this gesture as an insincere promise, workers in most of Russia began to return to work. Soon, the St. Petersburg soviet was forced to call off the strike although it demonstrated its influence by having all 200,000 workers report to work at the same time. Further strikes for the eight-hour day and against the execution of Kronstadt sailors were to show the potential power of the small but highly centralized Russian working class. This experiment in grass roots democracy was ended with the arrest of the soviet leadership in St. Petersburg on December 3 while Moscow was quieted by the middle of the month. This defeat was inevitable since the council movement had been limited to the urban areas and especially to the proletarian stronghold of St. Petersburg.

The Left and the Council Movement

The Russian left, such as it was in 1905, was as taken aback by the creation of soviets as was the Czarist government. Most prominent socialists were in exile and did not return in time to play any significant role. Many, particularly at first the Bolsheviks, saw no need for the existence of the councils. They regarded the political party as the natural leadership structure for workers and resented the soviets as rivals. Others maintained that the soviets were little more than a broader type of trade union strike support committee. Ultimately, most factions of the left participated in the soviets although they were never to control them. The reality that the soviets represented a form of direct, grassroots democracy that went beyond any particular political party or trade union was, at best, only faintly perceived by most professional revolutionaries.

In addition, most socialists believed that any future Russian revolution would be "bourgeois." Simply put, they thought that the new post-revolutionary society would be capitalistic and run roughly along the lines of the United States, France or Great Britain. Unlike in other European nations, the middle class liberals in Russia supported the notion of revolution and actively opposed the czarist regime. Since it was the prevailing wisdom, among liberals and Marxists alike, that any successful revolution would lead to a western-style bourgeois parliamentary system, the significance of the soviets was generally overlooked. That is, given the backwardness of the country, virtually no one thought Russia was economically or socially ready for socialism. The only system which was generally seen as viable in Russia was capitalism, which most socialists hoped would prepare the ground for a future socialist society. Thus, even worker's councils were considered useful pressure groups against czarism, but not vehicles for socialist revolution. Unusual in his perspective, even among the Bolsheviks, was Lenin. The Bolshevik leader realized that unlike western Europe, Russia's bourgeoisie was too weak to make a revolution on its own. Therefore, the small but concentrated proletariat would have to make the revolution and, hence, the vital importance of soviets. Like Lenin, Trotsky was another individual who appreciated the potential power of the councils. The most renowned leader of the St. Petersburg soviet in 1905, Trotsky would later join with Lenin in 1917 to mobilize the soviets as a revolutionary force.

Given the historical strength of anarchism in Russia, the fatherland of Bakunin and Kropotkin, it would not have been surprising if anarchists played an important revolutionary role. Furthermore, all the circumstances of Russian political life—the lack of civil liberties, the absence of parliamentary democracy, and the low level of education—should have placed anarchists in a position of spontaneous leadership of the mass rebellion. In actuality, with a few insignificant exceptions, anarchism was without influence or effect. The anarchists largely ignored the soviets, ridiculing them as bourgeois institutions unworthy of revolutionary support.

Instead of enhancing the strength of the anarchist movement, the events of 1905 severely damaged its reputation. This is particularly so because "anarchism" or "anarcho-communism" were phrases commonly used by dubious individuals to justify what amounted to little more than theft and robbery. Further, the anarchist movement failed to recruit a mass base of support despite considerable effort to do so. Marxist Rosa Luxemburg went so far as to assert that the events in 1905 had ruined anarchism as a mass movement since criminal elements used it as a cover while, like a school of sharks, they "swarm in the wake of the battleship of revolution."

Mass Strike

Although the question of general strikes had been extensively debated before 1905, the importance of the mass strikes in Russia raised the question anew for the European left. For syndicalists, the experience of Russia confirmed the correctness of their theories. In both France and Italy, where significant syndicalist movements existed, there was great excitement at the Russian example of mass strikes being used as offensive weapons against the government. Many in the more revolutionary wing of the Second International saw the mass strike as a new weapon that could be employed against reaction in a time of popular unrest.

In point of fact, mass strikes were undertaken in a number of European nations before 1914. Sweden saw the trade union movement use a general strike in 1909 in response to an employer's offense against labor. Despite considerable international support, especially from workers in Denmark and Norway, the strike was broken after a month with the socialists and trade unions losing over half their membership. Still within two years, the Swedish left had regrouped and doubled their number in the parliament in the 1911 election. In Belgium in April 1913, workers were called off the job as a protest against the unfair electoral system and only returned when the government agreed to revise the constitution.

Most socialists, however, were afraid to threaten the mass strike for a number of practical reasons. First, they feared that talk of a general strike would open them to a new wave of government repression. Caution was clearly the predominant mood among German socialists, who always looked over their shoulders in fear of new anti-socialist laws. When the Germans were criticized for their timidity at the 1907 Stuttgart Congress, August Bebel immediately pointed out that no less than three members of the editorial staff of the SPD's *Leipziger Volkszeitung* (*Leipzig People's Paper*) sat in the Kaiser's prisons.

Another reason for this reluctance to embrace the mass strike was the existence of relatively free elections and (at least basic) civil liberties in the west. Many radicals were so wedded to the concept of a parliamentary road to socialism that they could not envision a situation when a mass strike would actually be needed. In backward Russia, the mass strike made perfect sense, these radicals would say, but in the west they regarded the circumstances as completely different.

Finally, there was, of course, the fear that a mass strike would be a mass failure. Socialists who had seen steady increases in membership, influence, and votes were extremely hesitant to wager everything on one roll of the historical dice. The head of the German unions called the general strike "general nonsense." People such as him asked what if workers did not respond to a call for a general strike. What if the strike is defeated, and the capitalists use it as an excuse to destroy our movement?

Not only Russians like Lenin but also Rosa Luxemburg answered all these objections. In her *The Mass Strike, the Political Party and the Trade Unions* written immediately after the 1905 Revolution, Luxemburg argued that a genuine strike movement growing out of a situation of rebellion and serving as a means of struggle was far different from the earlier anarchist or syndicalist wishful thinking. For her, the mass strike was a democratic expression of the will of the people, which was far more active and empowering than the more passive act of merely voting for parliamentary candidates. In addition, Luxemburg argued, general strikes created viable revolutionary organization in a spontaneous yet democratic fashion. For Luxemburg, the mass strike was the missing link between the belief that revolution can just be proclaimed, held by some on the "infantile" left, and the growing conservatism of mainstream radical institutions like unions.

Road to War

In spite of all the discussions of how war could be averted, there existed widespread disbelief that the peace would be broken. While nearly everyone in Europe acknowledged the possibility of a massive armed conflict, few actually felt one would occur, at least before the summer of 1914. Peace had become the normal condition for the generation before World War I. Since the defeat of Napoleon at Waterloo in 1815, there had been no European-wide war. The last armed conflict between major European powers had ended in 1871 with the conclusion of the Franco-Prussian war and the unification of Germany. What conflicts had taken place had been overseas or at the far reaches of the European world such as the Russo-Japanese war, the Russo-Turkish War or the Balkan Wars.

As the major European powers drifted towards war in 1914, most Europeans expected the conflict to be deflected. Until the actual outbreak of hostilities, and sometimes even after, the average European simply could not believe war would take place. Yet, the evidence pointing to the impending mass slaughter was there for all to see. For the better part of a decade before, the major European powers had been dividing themselves into increasingly hostile alliances. On one side stood England, France, Russia and a host of lesser nations while on the other Germany, the Austro-Hungarian Empire, the Ottoman Empire and a few others. These alliances severely limited flexibility in times of a political crisis since loyalty to one alliance took precedence over all other considerations.

Not only was Europe divided into two camps but each camp was steadily increasing its arms. As fear and distrust had become the norm in relations between European governments, each began making immense armaments purchases. As more and more of a nation's wealth was devoted to instruments of war, ironically the less secure each country's rulers felt. The cost of all these new guns, ships and army units can be measured by the per capita military expenditure of the major powers. Great Britain, which spent only $3.46 a person on weapons of war in 1880, was disbursing $8.23 per capita by 1914. Likewise, France, which had given $4.02 a person to armaments in 1880, gave $7.07 by the start of the First World War. On the other side, Imperial Germany had only spent $2.16 per capita on the tools of war in 1880 but by 1914 was spending $8.19 per citizen. Even the relatively poor Austro-Hungarian Empire increased armaments expenditures from $1.70 per capita in 1880 to $3.10 a person by 1914.

While it would be tempting to blame the "military-industrial complex" of plotting the war, there is no evidence to prove the armament manufacturers wanted a war, as some radicals have charged. What they wanted were arms sales and the profits which went with them. That this arms race contributed to the war is true, but the capitalists were concerned with profits, not fighting. Although the buildup of armaments may have increased the likelihood of war, this was a mere side effect of the main goal, which was to increase profits through lucrative government contracts.

The cause of the war was far less conspiratorial and less direct. Essentially, a situation existed were the major powers drifted into a war which few really wanted and most refused to believe would happen even if they feared it was inevitable. As economic competition had sharpened between the major European powers, most had gone overseas to search for militarily weaker peoples to colonize. Once the non-European world was divided up, the rivalry between nations and the underlying economic competition did not go away. On the contrary, it grew more intense. With the overlap of economic interests and politico-military power, many nations felt compelled to defend "their" interests even at the risk of threatening armed conflict. This is not surprising since one of the uses for military might was to protect and expand economic advantage. To do any less would have meant accepting a status as a second rate power. The economic basis of the war was widely accepted by observers of all political tendencies at the time. As Woodrow Wilson (1856–1924), 28th President of the United States noted in a speech in St. Louis, "is there any man here or any woman—let me say, is there any child here—who does not know that the seed of war in the modern world is commercial and industrial rivalry?"

As the seemingly hopelessly confused (and confusing) situation in the Balkans drew the attention of, first, the Austro-Hungarian Empire and czarist Russia and, thereafter, all their respective allies, Europe stumbled towards war in the summer of 1914. War could have been avoided but that would have required government leaders more willing to act than react. Often, the leaders were not entirely sure a war would be such a bad thing. Many thought a short (and naturally victorious) war might help them. Some in the British Admiralty hoped to teach Germany a lesson about the dangers of challenging the Royal Navy's supremacy. The French wanted the return of Alsace-Lorraine while German nationalists sought a "place in the sun." Russia wanted to expand into the Balkans while the rulers in

Vienna sought to destroy Slavic nationalism and establish themselves as the power in the Balkans. Even those who did not want war could see the impending war as possibly useful.

European Radicals and the Impending War

On June 28, 1914, a Serbian nationalist assassinated the Austrian Archduke Franz Ferdinand and his wife in the Bosnian town of Sarajevo. Russia's ally Serbia was implicated in this act of murder, and, in any event, the Austro-Hungarian government had been looking for a reason to take action against the Serbian government and the troublesome Slavs nationalists it encouraged. It was believed, in the highest circles in Vienna, that firm action against Serbia would do much to restore calm among the Empire's restless ethnic minorities. The Archduke's assassination set off the chain of events which resulted in the First World War. Initially, the European left did not appear unduly concerned. At first, no one expected a war since assassinations had taken place any number of times in previous years without the result of armed conflict. Further, if a war broke out, most thought that it would be limited to fighting in the Balkans, a mysterious region known to most only from adventure or children's books.

The leaders of the Socialist International, in fact, saw no reason why they should disrupt their summer vacation plans over a crisis which would surely blow over. So, Kautsky went on holiday to Rome, Austrian socialist Viktor Adler to Bad Nauheim and even Lenin took his ill wife to the Carpathians for her health. By late July, as the Austrian ultimatum to Serbia, which amounted to little more than a polite request for the Serbians to commit political suicide, showed the real danger of war erupting, the radical press duly condemned the preparations for war. "No drop of a German soldier's blood must be sacrificed to the Austrian despots' lust for power," the SPD executive appeal to German workers read, "We want no war! Down with war!"

When news of the Austrian ultimatum reached Jean Jaurès, he praised the editorials in the German socialist *Vorwärts* and gave speeches telling his listeners that socialism "represents the only promise of a possibility of peace." From July 26 till 30, massive peace rallies were held throughout Germany. When on July 29, an emergency meeting of the Socialist International was convened in Brussels, many would still not believe that war was imminent. Adler, for the Austrian socialists, began the meeting on an extremely depressing note by stating that the left in his country was helpless. The mobilization of the army had begun, martial law had been imposed, and there was a rising wave of patriotism sweeping across Vienna.

Other delegates had little better to report. "What can we do?" a delegate from Prague noted in despair, "Parliament is suspended and public meetings prohibited. Anyone who resists mobilization will be hanged." The mood was considerably improved when Germany's Hugo Haase (1863–1919) recounted the size and frequency of peace demonstrations in his nation. Moreover, Haase raised hopes when he said positively, but incorrectly, that the "Kaiser is against the war, not for humanitarian reasons but simply from fear." In the same vein, Jaurès argued that the French government wanted peace and that it was only up to the socialists to pressure them into restraining the Czar. From Great Britain, Keir Hardie added that it was "out of the question" for his country to join in any possible war. Thus, as the meeting ended that evening with a public demonstration for peace attended by thousands of Belgian workers, the leaders of the Socialist International felt it possible, perhaps likely, that war would be avoided. Without any practical alternative, they were content to continue their fight through their press and by mass meetings against war.

The non-socialist left was equally mobilized against the outbreak of armed conflict. Both anarchists and syndicalists throughout Europe let it be known that war would be met with massive resistance. "Workers must answer any declaration of war," announced the CGT's *La Bataille Syndicaliste* on July 26, "by a revolutionary general strike." The secretary of the CGT even attempted to ask Karl Legien (1861–1920) of the German trade unions if his members would join a general strike against the war. The German's response was a diplomatic silence.

5. From War to Revolution, Europe 1914–1917

When war was finally declared in the first days of August 1914, many expected at least an attempt, however symbolic it might prove to be, at resistance from the left. Firmly opposed to war in principle and having violently condemned the coming of this war specifically, many people from all strata of society expected substantial antiwar activities. In France, for instance, the government anticipated that as many as 13 percent of those called to arms would attempt to dodge the draft. Almost everyone on the left predicted that the German socialists in the Reichstag would follow the example of Wilhelm Liebknecht and August Bebel during the Franco-Prussian war and refuse to vote for war credits.

What shocked all but the most cynical radicals was the outbreak of patriotic enthusiasm which greeted a war which would leave nearly 20 million Europeans dead or disabled before it ended. Across Europe, governments were mistaken when they assumed widespread repression would be necessary to put down antiwar militants. The onset of the war caused no general strikes, no insurrection, not much draft resistance, and even Russia experienced only a few thousand resisters in place of the upwards of a million that the Czar's officials had predicted. Although this lack of resistance was to quickly dissipate, the people of Europe—and along with them the bulk of the European left—went lightheartedly to kill and be killed.

The German Social Democrats voted for war credits (which so astounded Lenin when he first read of it, he assumed it was a fabrication) as did the French socialists and almost everyone else, save a few delegates to the Czar's Duma (and those German socialists who went to the bathroom in order to miss the vote on war credits). Why this sudden and unexpected change of heart? Fear was certainly a factor.

The European left, both the socialists in parliament and the syndical-ist trade unionists, had little desire to face government persecution or be forced underground. After all, they had made impressive strides in the past generation and were loath to give their enemies the opportu-nity to drive them underground. Their organizations, newspapers, buildings and other physical property holdings were all hostages to their rulers.

Yet it would be unduly cynical to place prime emphasis on the radical's self interest as the reason for the movement's acquiescence to the war. Revolutionaries had shown before 1914 and would show again later the risks they were willing to take and the hardships they would undergo for the sake of their beliefs. There was, however, a lack of leadership at the time the war broke out. Marx, Engels, Wilhelm Liebknecht, to mention but a few, were long dead. Ger-many's Bebel had died the year before the war. Jaurès, who had threatened to continue the fight for peace once the shooting started and might have rallied other antiwar socialists, was assassinated by a hysterical nationalist only days before the fighting began. There was no one in the socialist world, or for that matter the left as a whole, who had the authority which might have kept radicals from caving into the tremendous pressure felt during those days.

Any hope of sustained anarchist reaction was hampered by that movement's weakness and the support for the war by its most prominent leader—Kropotkin. In Italy, where the PSI had remained faithful to their antiwar principles, a mainly anarcho-syndicalist group left the party to support the war. By late 1914, Italian syndical-ists who supported the notion of a "revolutionary war" had organ-ized themselves into the *Fasci di Azione Revoluzionaria* (Bands of Revolutionary Action) which were soon to be led by Benito Mussolini. Thus, the members of all tendencies within the European radical movement witnessed how the allure of nationalism drew large sections of the common people into support for the war.

Moreover, most leftists convinced themselves that they were only supporting a war of defense. This had been one of the glaring prob-lems which had arisen during previous discussions on the possibility of war. Opposing a blatantly aggressive war was quite different, in the minds of these leftists, than defending their own nation which was under attack. Thus, French militants went off to war reassured that they were fighting to save their homes from the German invader. In Germany, as soon as Russia entered the conflict, the historical abhorrence for czarism was translated into a feeling that this was war against "barbarism." The bulk of the Labour Party in Great Britain backed the war to defend civilization from the "Hun." Among those nations at war only in Russia and poor, tiny Serbia did a significant number of citizens reject the war when it first broke out. The widespread belief that the war was defensive took a great significance later when the less than noble goals of governmental officials on all sides became known.

Nor was this capitulation to war fever the preserve of leaders alone. The average European, and even European radical, was carried away with patriotic frenzy in August 1914. The same people who so passionately screamed "Down with war!" only days earlier were convinced that the war was defensive, necessary, and supportable. Still, it was men more than women, the middle class more than workers who welcomed the start of this conflict. Nevertheless, seldom has a war in this century received such an enthusiastic send off.

Finally, even the most revolutionary of antiwar proponents lacked a workable strategy to stop a war. Despite syndicalist calls for a general strike and socialist proclamations of international solidarity, the left had nothing approaching an alternative plan to prevent the efforts of governments that were preparing for war. Perhaps most leftists had never really expected that a war to come. Others, particularly anarchists, thought the masses would never allow a war to take place. The hitherto powerful movements of opposition would be rendered, however temporarily, impotent in face of armed conflict between nations. Even those who remained opposed to the war were momentarily resigned to their fate since, as the Czech socialist had asked, what could they do?

World War's Impact on Europe

When the soldiers marched away in August 1914, most of them thought the war would be over by Christmas and, of course, that their side would be victorious. As it turns out, the war was to last until the late Autumn of 1918 and leave unforeseen millions of victims in its wake. The left, unable to stop the war, at first underestimated its impact. The normally overzealous British anarchist journal *Freedom,* which could be expected to paint matters as darkly as possible, was content to predict "tens of thousands" would die. Many socialists and other radicals thought that the war would soon be over, and they could get back to business as usual.

As the war dragged on with a higher level of killing than most had foreseen, the mood rapidly changed. As war fever cooled down and the number of volunteers dropped, men who found themselves in uniform were mainly unwilling draftees. By the end of the war in 1918, a larger proportion of men would serve in the armed forces than in any previous conflict. By the time the October 1917 Revolution pulled Russia out of the war, some 15.3 million people had been utilized in the military out of a population of just over 139 million. This was far from unique as Germany enlisted a little over 11 million out of a population of just under 65 million, while France with a populace of 39 million used 8.3 million people. These numbers illustrate that a rather extraordinarily large percentage of the adult, particularly male, population was directly involved in the conflict through military service.

Further, unlike previous wars, this contest was to directly affect civilians—it would reach the so-called home front. Not only would noncombatants be touched by fighting taking place in their regions, which has always been the case, but civilians were also affected by the strain the war would place on the domestic economy. By the end of the war, there would be many cases of virtual starvation because enough food to adequately feed civilians was either unavailable (Germany as a result of the British naval blockade) or could not be shipped to many areas because of the transportation collapse caused by the war (Russia). Seldom, if ever, had a war caused such profound consequences for so many Europeans.

Before long, the governments involved naturally invoked every available means to win this all-out effort. In France, the mobilization of so many men for the army created a huge labor shortage which was partially alleviated by forcing many remaining workers to work twelve hours shifts. After December 5, 1916, all German men not in uniform were bound to civilian war service. The press was severely censored in all the major nations: any unauthorized reports of French defeats becoming a crime, while German newspapers were forbidden to make reference to the fact that there was censorship. Even in traditionally liberal Great Britain, little real news reached the home front excepting that which came directly from soldiers on leave. Of course, there was never any question of press freedom in the Czar's Russia. What all government's shared was a tremendous fear that the average citizen would discover the actual conduct of the war and the true conditions at the front. "The people do not know what this war is like and they must not," British leader David Lloyd George (1863–1945) told the owner of the *Manchester Guardian*, "for if they did, they would stop it at once."

Women and the War

With such a multitude of men away at the front, women became the reserve army of labor that was mobilized to fill in the gaps left by departing male workers. Germany set up a women's service that established work shops in major urban areas where females would sew cartridge belts, uniforms, and hospital sheets. French women, besides knitting socks for the troops, took over a host of traditionally male occupations ranging from ploughing to repairing airplanes. In Great Britain, women constituted 60 per cent of all armament workers with many working twelve hours a day—every day.

Although by the end of the war, women could be found in all types of jobs previously reserved for men, they were invariably paid less. Women in most European armaments factories usually made half what their male counterparts earned for the same work. More-

over, while women worked in any number of very visible occupations, such as bus drivers, they continued to be excluded from most
positions of influence. Moreover, there was not only discrimination
but also sexual harassment of female workers. In France, for instance,
women employed in both textiles and armaments were forced to go
on strike because of sexual harassment. This should come as no
surprise as many males were uncomfortable with female factory work,
while the nation's right wing issued postcards urging young French
women to fulfill their patriotic duty, to "make love," in order to
produce the next generation of soldiers.

Still, in spite of the sexist attitudes of male dominated society,
women's status changed during the war. Because it was not practical
for women working in war industries to wear corsets or complex
hairdos, women began to wear shorter skirts, bobbed hair and looser
clothing. It became commonplace for women to wear makeup and to
go out unchaperoned. When food shortages began to radicalize the
urban population, it was women who stood out as the most vocal
protesters. In fact, the first significant civil disturbances were food
riots comprised of angry women. Ironically, the necessities of war
caused women to gain many rights that the left had long championed,
including the vote in Germany, Austria, Sweden, Luxembourg, and
the Netherlands. Among many working class women a greater
interest in politics in general, and radical politics in specific, grew out
of these developments.

Casualties during the War

After the war was in full swing, all sides used massive human wave
assaults in a vain attempt to break through enemy positions and turn
the stalemate into a victory. These ill-advised attacks did not produce
a victory. What these assaults did achieve was the most massive
destruction of human life then seen on European soil. 1916 was to be
the bloodiest year of the war. In a series of battles which were to have
little bearing on the ultimate outcome of the conflict, soldiers were
thrown against enemy positions with horrifying results. War had

become as industrialized as the societies which fought it. The defensive weapons of war, from machine guns which allowed a few men to quickly kill hundreds, to poison gas which often failed to discriminate between friend and foe, proved far stronger than the bravery of charging human beings. The field marshals and generals refused to concede that spirit was no match for technology, and millions paid for this refusal.

The Russian Brusilov offensive of June-July 1916 cost nearly a million men. In the same year, during the battle of the Somme, the British sustained 419,000 casualties, the French 204,000, and Germany about half a million. Meanwhile, after the 1916 battle of Verdun, with 420,000 individuals killed and yet another 800,000 wounded or afflicted by poison gas, there were over 150,000 mangled bodies whose identities could not be determined. While the creation of this mountain of corpses did nothing to end the war, it did much to invigorate antiwar radicals and lead to a revitalized, revolutionary left. No longer would the idea of a shorter or relatively painless war lull revolutionaries into inaction. What for some had been mainly a question of abstract principles became a matter of life and death. In terms of human and material resources, the war was to push the major European powers to the breaking point—and in the case of Russia, at least, beyond. This weakening of the institutions of the status quo was to provide the revolutionary left with an opportunity—however fleeting—to reshape society.

Inception of Antiwar Activism

Until the war, leftists had considered armed conflict as only one more example of the fearful results of capitalism's imperialistic nature. They had all pledged themselves, in one manner or another, "to wage war on war." Once the war had begun, radicals as diverse as Russian anarchist Peter Kropotkin, who called upon all "lovers of human progress" to crush Germany, and British socialist, Belfort Bax (1854–1926), who wrote that the German SPD leadership were traitors to humanity, devoted their efforts to helping their side win. Although the entire weight of prewar radical literature (most clearly the idea of international class solidarity) pledged that radicals would work for an end to any future war, most sought to justify their pro-war conduct by blaming the conflict exclusively upon the "enemy."

Thus, the war not only split Europe into warring camps, it additionally split the radical movement. Besides those pro-war militants who increasingly muted their antagonism to their own rulers in support of the war effort, there remained radicals in the neutral European nations. In these nations, the pressure to capitulate to nationalism under the guise of self-defense was far weaker. Thus, with the outbreak of the war, socialists and other leftists in Sweden, Denmark, Italy, the Netherlands, Spain, Romania, and Bulgaria protested against any attempt to involve their country in the fighting. In Italy, the PSI went so far as to menace the government with the threat of an armed uprising if it honored treaty obligations and joined the German attack on France.

Within a month of the start of the hostilities, the American Socialist Party requested a meeting of socialists of all nations to work out a common policy to speedily end the fighting. This initiative was doomed when the French and Belgian socialists refused to attend the same meeting as Germans, who had failed to protest the invasion of their territory. Thus, when the conference took place in neutral Copenhagen on January 17, 1915, only the socialist parties of Sweden, Norway, Denmark, and the Netherlands along with delegates from Russia's Jewish Bund attended. In February, the socialists from the allied countries met in London while the German, Austrian, and Hungarian socialists gathered in Vienna during April. In both cases, although the assemblies dutifully professed their loyalty to socialism and the principle of self-determination, the thrust of the meetings reaffirmed support for the war. This meant that a common program for peace was, for the moment at least, out of the question.

Already the dangers of tying ostensibly revolutionary movements to the war-imposed demand for national unity was being voiced by an antiwar minority. At the London conference, a minority, including the secretary of the French Metalworkers' Union, argued that socialists needed to regain their political independence while the Bolsheviks demanded that all alliances with bourgeois parties be dissolved and war credits opposed. In Imperial Germany, the unanimity of Reichstag support for war credits disappeared as early as December 1914 when Karl Liebknecht voted "Nein" in spite of the coercion exercised by party officials.

Nor was he alone in his opposition after a small group formed which opposed the war and which also included Rosa Luxemburg, Franz Mehring (1846–1919), and Clara Zetkin. Even the pressure of western socialists to convince the Italian left to support Italian entry into the war on the side of France and England was unable to sway the bulk of the PSI from their antiwar attitude. All in the all, the cracks within the pro-war facade were seemingly widening each week that the war continued. As it turned out, the European left would undergo a schism generated by the hostilities unleashed by the war, particularly after 1917 which would splinter the radical movement for the rest of the century.

Zimmerwald

In an attempt to break the deadlock that the socialist movement faced with regards to the war, the Italian and Swiss parties decided to initiate an international conference in autumn 1915. The expressed purpose of this assembly was to call on the proletariat to form a united front for peace while providing a focal point for antiwar activists. All members of the working class movement who rejected a political truce with their rulers were summoned to help formulate a common international campaign in opposition to the bloodshed. Naturally, this meant excluding the bulk of socialists in belligerent countries who supported their government's conduct.

Despite the obvious limitation such a restriction placed on the gathering which met at Zimmerwald, Switzerland in September 1915, the conference was of great relevance. In fact, it is amazing such a meeting occurred at all. After all, the dangers of participation, let alone the difficulty in reaching Zimmerwald could have easily derailed the proposed gathering. Yet, a number of important and well-known radicals attended in order to openly announce their hatred for the bloodshed which had become a daily a part of European life. At the very moment when their countrymen were killing each other, French and German labor leaders could shake hands and declare that this was not their war.

Although only thirty-eight delegates attended, the symbolic importance of Zimmerwald should not be underestimated. While the only parties officially represented were the PSI and parties from Eastern Europe such as Lenin's Bolsheviks, participants included activists from Germany, France, Sweden, and Holland. Although the Swiss did not officially endorse the conference, they were represented, and Robert Grimm (1881–1958) editor of their *Berner Tagwacht* was one of the principal organizers. The Independent Labour Party and the British Socialist Party had attempted to send delegates but were refused passports by their government. The final conference manifesto, in which the delegates demanded a peace settlement without annexations or reparations based on the right of nations to self-determination, was adopted unanimously. The text of the Zimmerwald declaration appeared in the radical press of neutral countries, Great Britain and Italy. In addition, it circulated covertly throughout France, Germany, and Russia.

The unity of the Zimmerwald participants had not come easily. Lenin had introduced a resolution calling on the gathering to devote itself to turning the imperialist war into a civil war. Further, he wished a decisive split from the old International and all those who had supported the war. Lenin's demands for revolutionary action fell mainly on deaf ears as he was able to muster only seven votes out of the thirty-eight representatives present. The majority had no desire to create a new international organization or push for insurrection. Rather, despite Lenin's threats to vote against the final manifesto, they wished to launch a broad-based movement which would reject the notion of a "social truce" while compelling their respective governments to end the warfare. Their two goals were, therefore, to restore working class militancy and fight for peace. Notwithstanding Lenin's defeat, his position at Zimmerwald was a harbinger of Bolshevik actions to come.

While the Zimmerwald call to the "Proletariat of Europe" helped expand the influence of antiwar sentiment, the bulk of the pro-war radicals were unmoved by the breach in their ranks. The leaders of the Second International maintained that the Zimmerwald group represented little beyond their own opinions and urged members to spurn their advances. To counter the charge that they were generals without troops, the Zimmerwald committee organized a second conference which assembled in April 1916 in the Swiss village of Canthal. While forty-four delegates attended this time, they represented more or less the same organizations as before, although the Swiss party was officially represented and a leader of French syndicalism was in attendance.

Once more, Lenin came to the conference prepared for battle, and, once more, was he defeated. The Bolshevik leader called antiwar propaganda a sham unless it called on the troops to lay down their arms. Further, he continued to argue for a break with the old leaders of the European left. Of the forty-four people present, this program of revolutionary propaganda and a break with the past leadership received but twelve votes. That the gathering had not come together to split from the old International was illustrated by the speech given by Giacinto Serrati (1872–1926) who on behalf of the seven member Italian delegation declared that they would withdraw from the meeting if Lenin's proposals were approved.

In the end, unity was maintained and a proclamation issued again. The text was largely the same as the 1915 manifesto except that the conference demanded that socialists refuse all support for the war including the voting of war credits. Pro-war forces predictably dismissed the second conference as meaningless, yet the "Zimmerwald movement" was becoming the tip of ever growing iceberg of antiwar sentiment. In the atmosphere of war, the idea of an international peace meeting took on far more political—and psychological—significance than it might otherwise have.

Divisions within Radical Organizations

Within each country, the left splintered over the question of supporting its nation's war effort. Almost with each passing week, support for the conflict softened as antiwar feeling grew. In Great Britain, the socialist Independent Labour Party, which was part of the larger Labour Party, rejected support for the war from the beginning of the war. When the mainstream labor movement allowed union officials to join a unity government, the ILP condemned the move but refrained from seceding from the Labour Party.

During the first nine months or so of the war, the French left uttered no sign of protest. More strongly than most, French radicals viewed the conflict as being a matter of self-defense against German aggression. This homogeneity was broken on May Day 1915 when the Metal Workers Union published a declaration of international solidarity in their publication, *Union des Métaux*. The secretary of this union and a leading member of the CGT, Alphonse Merrheim (1881–1925) participated in the Zimmerwald conference and formed the *Comité pour la Reprise des Rélations Internationales* (Committee for the Resumption of International Relations), which was to be the core of opposition to the war. Soon after the Committee's formation, the Teachers' Union joined, and its journal *L'École de la fédération* became the periodical of the Zimmerwald movement in France.

Within the French socialist party, opposition was slower in developing largely because any revolutionary mass movement against the government would offer, the socialists believed, the Germans an opportunity to seize Paris. Nonetheless, as the slaughter continued, the socialist antiwar minority increased in strength. A resolution for a peace campaign received a mere seventy-six votes at the party's December 1915 congress yet a year later a similar motion lost by the narrow margin of 1,437 to 1,407. As elsewhere in Europe, the minority desired neither to split the party nor provoke a civil war.

Unlike France, there was not a single square inch of German soil under foreign occupation. Therefore, the argument that the war was a defensive one was harder to peddle. Increasingly it appeared to the masses as a naked war of conquest. Thus, from the first shot fired, there was opposition to the policy of Kaiser Wilhelm II and his government. While Karl Liebknecht was the first to publicly proclaim himself an enemy of war and the class truce, he was certainly not the last. In February 1915, Liebknecht led the majority of the SPD members in the Prussian legislature in condemning the "policy of August 4th." A few months later, an open letter to the SPD leadership, which demanded an end to the political truce, bore the signatures of more than 1,000 important party members.

By 1916, in spite of governmental pressure (martial law and press censorship) and SPD party discipline, the bulk of the antiwar minority, who had kept their mouths shut, could no longer bear to remain silent. When Emergency War Credits were asked of the Reichstag in March, the SPD minority decided to vote "*Nein.*" Hugo Haase was chosen to explain their condemnation of aggressive war aims and the "State of Emergency." His speech was never finished because it caused a great tumult among those present, and the Reichstag voted to forbid him from speaking further. Afterwards, Haase and his group were expelled from the SPD's Reichstag delegation (although they remained party members), so they formed their own parliamentary group which was later to be the nucleus of the Independent Social Democratic Party (USPD).

Haase and Georg Ledebour (1850–1947) continued their fight within the party and received about 40 percent of the votes for their resolutions at the September 1916 SPD national conference. A large majority of the antiwar members of the party made efforts to avoid a split within Germany's socialist organization. Yet, without a universally revered leader like the late August Bebel to maintain unity, the conflict became ever more bitter. Finally, in January 1917, the party leadership expelled all local branches which sided with the opposition. In April, a gathering of antiwar activists met at Gotha and formed the Independent Social Democratic Party, the left-wing of which was later to become the German Communist Party (KPD).

The situation was far different in Austria. In contrast to Germany, the government had suspended the parliament in the spring of 1914, and it was not reconvened until May 1917. Rather than publicly back the war, Austrian radicals mainly kept silent. Mostly, the mood was of resignation. One notable exception was Friedrich Adler (1879–1960) who protested against the passivity of the party which was led by his father. In October 1916, the younger Adler assassinated the Prime Minister as a protest against the war. Still, the mass of Austrians remained glum but quiet. The situation changed in 1917 under the dual impact of the March revolution in Russia and Friedrich Adler's rousing speech during his trial in May. From then on, antiwar activity expanded, it appeared, daily.

As the carnage on the battlefields of Europe continued, more and more people demanded an end to the conflict. In addition to the mass murder of the war, the left and their working class followers were enraged at the ghastly sacrifices, both material (food shortages, falling real wages) and political (class truce and censorship), demanded of those at home. Except for Lenin's Bolsheviks and relatively small groups in the west, however, what most socialists wanted was peace and a return to prewar revolutionary struggle not an immediate insurrection or a civil war. In the world of czarist Russia, the situation was to turn out quite differently.

March Revolution in Russia

On March 8, 1917 (actually February 23 in Russia since they still used the Julian calendar), female textile workers, who performed unskilled labor for as long as twelve hours before going home to do housework, in Petrograd (St. Petersburg had been renamed) went on strike against the deplorable shortage of bread. Little more than ten days worth of flour had remained in the city in the previous weeks, and the threat of mass starvation loomed large. The female strikers rallied support from other women whom they met in markets and bread lines. By the next day, half the industrial labor force was on strike, and Cossack soldiers refused to fire on crowds of workers. Within a week the last remaining troops had surrendered, and Czar Nicholas II abdicated. A provisional government was quickly established to rule Russia until elections could be held.

Once more, soviets (councils) sprang up in Petrograd and throughout the country. On March 27, the Petrograd soviet issued a manifesto calling upon the workers of the world to join together in a common campaign for a peace without annexations. Yet, at the same time, there was the provisional government consisting of liberal politicians. Russia had in effect two systems of government: one the traditional parliamentary government which looked to western nations as a model and the other, this new council system organized from the bottom of society upward. It was a situation of dual power.

The Russian left, including the Bolsheviks, was dazed by the speed of events. At first, the Provisional Government was received with such euphoria that its support was all but universal, for even the Bolshevik's *Pravda* (*Truth*) supported it on all basic actions. Not until several months later when Lenin was able to convince his party to move into opposition was there any organized dissent. There were good reasons for this initial support. The government had instituted reforms of the military and purged many monarchist officers. The government pledged itself to the democratization of Russian political life with the promise of free elections and the granting of basic civil liberties. It disestablished the Russian Orthodox Church and ended legal discrimination against ethnic minorities. None of these measures were a small matter in a country with a tradition as historically oppressive as Russia.

All the same, this new temporary government (it was to hold power only until elections could be held) was basically bourgeois and as such, it was tied to the concept of property rights. This meant that it could not take the drastic measures required if it were to continue to enjoy the population's favor. Specifically, while the Provisional Government nationalized the lands of the Czar's family, it would not condone further expropriations. When land hungry peasants seized land on their own initiative, the government sent troops to disperse the rural "squatters."

The government's dilemma was much the same in the urban areas. Although it expressed sympathy for the plight of industrial workers (and as later events would show, needed their backing), in practice, it fought against wage demands and a relaxation of labor discipline. Within six months of the March revolution, it reestablished the right of owners to fire workers and deduct pay for meetings held during working hours. By the fall, Alexander Kerensky (1881–1970), the most prominent leader of the Provisional Government, demonstratively selected the head of the Moscow Stock Exchange to coordinate economic policy. Even the largely symbolic plea that May Day become a national holiday was rejected by the probusiness government.

Perhaps most fatefully, and in contradiction to statements about wanting a peace as outlined by the Zimmerwald conference, Kerensky and the Provisional Government kept Russia in the war. There were many reasons behind this politically suicidal decision. Ironically, Kerensky's government hoped that the continuation of warfare would unite the country and reduce the social conflict which was ripping Russia apart. In addition, the leaders of the Provisional Government identified with the western capitalist governments and were hesitant to abandon them in their hour of need. Further, leaving aside all questions of sentiment, the Provisional Government felt that it needed the west economically. That is, it counted on massive western financial aid and investment to turn backward Russia into a modern capitalist nation like France or the United States. If the leaders of the Provisional Government unilaterally concluded a peace with Germany, they knew, and were bluntly told by western ambassadors, that no money would be forthcoming after the war.

All Power to the Soviets

If the Provisional Government had faced only disorganized or splintered opposition, it might still have survived long enough for Germany's final defeat and western aid to rescue it. In point of fact, since its establishment, the Provisional Government never had complete power. After all, the activities of the soviet movement represented a rival source of political power. As early as May 1917, there were 400 soviets throughout the old Russian Empire while by late fall 900 had been established. These councils represented not only urban workers but also peasants and more importantly, soldiers. In fact, soldiers tended to be extremely prominent in soviet movement of 1917.

In the absence of a democratically elected parliament, the soviets served as a type of revolutionary democracy complete with elections while delegates and office holders were subject to recall. Further, these councils were dominated by no one political party, but rather, represented a wide spectrum of opinions. While members of the soviets had not seen themselves as an alternative to a national parliament, by the fall of 1917 the Bolsheviks were advancing the slogan "All Power to the Soviets." The Bolsheviks believed was that the soviets could serve as an alternative model of democracy to the traditional parliamentary ideal. Many revolutionaries, like Trotsky, viewed the soviets as the embryo of popular self-government on the model of the Paris Commune. Although never fully developed, Lenin suggests this in his vision of the new society outlined in *State and Revolution*.

As summer turned to autumn, more and more urban councils, such as those in Moscow and Petrograd, elected Bolshevik majorities. Their campaign for "peace, land, and bread" was attracting new support daily, especially among politically active soviet members. Meanwhile, the Russian army was in the process of dissolving. Desertion and refusal to obey orders reached unheard of proportions. The soviet leadership issued Order Number One which authorized soldiers to elect their own councils, which would have the power to control all the weapons of their unit. In many regiments, officers who defied these soldier soviets risked being shot by their own men. When lulls in the fighting allowed, the demoralized Russian troops even fraternized with their German counterparts.

In the countryside, the peasantry became impatient with promises of land reform and began to seize the property of nobles and even that of the Russian Orthodox Church. As the Provisional Government attempted to prevent or overturn these land grabs, Kerensky and his ministers alienated many previously supportive peasants. By contrast, the Bolsheviks encouraged land seizures and urged the rural population to set up soviets to carry out land redistribution immediately. In general, the provisional government was a victim of her own errors.

Among these were not being tough enough to crush the Bolsheviks but being repressive enough to alienate sections of the population.

Bolsheviks Come to Power

In November 1917, as support for the Provisional Government had all but vanished, Lenin and Trotsky decided on a tremendous gamble: insurrection. With a party membership reaching a quarter of a million, widespread support in the armed forces and control of the key city soviets, the Bolsheviks had a formidable base of support. Still, they knew that they were a distinct minority among the most numerous class in Russian society, the peasantry. Further, backward Russia was hardly the ideal setting for constructing a socialist society, even in the best of times, and this certainly was not the best of times.

The idea of an insurrection was far from universally accepted within the Bolshevik party—not even in the Central Committee. In fact, Grigori Zinoviev (1883–1936) and Lev Kamenev (1883–1936), two leading Bolshevik Central Committee members, not only voted against the plan but announced their opposition publicly in the mainstream press. (Such was the nature of Bolshevik party democracy in those days that not even Lenin's fury was enough to have these two expelled). Again within the Petrograd city committee and other party organizations, Lenin's proposal won out, but not unanimously.

Why were Lenin, Trotsky, and the majority of Bolsheviks ready to risk everything on a gamble to seize power in such a devastated and backward country as Russia? To understand their reasoning, the context in which their decision was made must be understood. The massive slaughter taking place on the battlefields of Europe went on seemingly without end. Lenin and those who backed his decision to seize power believed that the war had created a situation where continent wide socialist revolution was imminent. Any break in the global chain of capitalism would hasten the coming of revolutions in other nations. Thus, the Bolshevik seizure of power would be but the first act in a European wide socialist transformation. Revolution was especially expected to be forthcoming in the powerful industrial giant of the Kaiser's Germany. The Bolshevik optimism was such Trotsky would later explain to a visiting U.S. businessman that Russia was the best country to invest in because, even after the American workers had expropriated his holdings at home, the soviet government would protect his investment in Russia.

Moreover, the Bolsheviks believed the capitalists would continue the war until a final victory by one side allowed it to impose a harsh and unfair peace on the vanquished. Therefore, it was thought that only socialist revolution could both end the war and lead to a just peace. Further, the tremendous suffering and destruction caused by the war had left Europe, and particularly Russia, in danger of utter material collapse. Only socialism would be able to repair the damage—both material and psychological—wrought by the capitalist bloodletting. Finally, the Bolsheviks believed that the failure to seize power would allow the far right to consolidate itself and reimpose an authoritarian regime on the peoples of Russia.

Kerensky and his Provisional Government, unpopular at home and isolated by the war from their foreign backers, were ripe for a revolutionary insurrection. The uprising was organized by Trotsky operating through the Petrograd Soviet's Military-Revolutionary Committee. In November, within a single day, the capital of Petrograd was seized with virtually no bloodshed as all strategic points were occupied while the precious few officers prepared to fight for the Provisional Government were disarmed and arrested. Kerensky himself fled in an American embassy staff car—an act emblematic of his lack of support, which also gave credence to the charge that he was a puppet of the western powers. In fact, much of the disaster was of his own design.

The All-Russia Congress of Soviets was presented with power, and Lenin addressed the assembly with the famous line: "We shall now proceed to construct the socialist order." Within twenty-four hours of seizing power, Lenin issued decrees on land reform and called for a cease fire with Germany. The message of the Bolshevik-dominated Congress was spread throughout Russia as soviets were encouraged to seize power, peasants told to take land and workers urged to seize their factories from the capitalists. The unthinkable had actually happened. A revolutionary socialist government now ruled a major European country. Its success depended on the revolution spreading, for as even Lenin acknowledged, "without Germany, we are lost."

The failure of the revolution elsewhere would doom the Bolshevik experiment to degenerate into a one person dictatorship under Stalin soon after Lenin's death in 1924. This dictatorship would murder almost all of the leaders who had led the revolution and would plunge Russia back into an age which can only be described as barbarous. Further, it would cause socialism and revolution to become words associated with dictatorship and brutality. At the end of 1917, however, the prospect for revolutionary success still appeared hopeful. Socialist victories which might have given Russia and the world a fate different from the horrors of Stalin's dictatorship.

6. Revolutionary Europe, 1917–1921

By the autumn of 1917, it was not only the Russian people who were suffering appallingly as the war dragged on into its fourth year. In the Kaiser's Germany, for one, the battlefield losses were staggering. By the end of what Woodrow Wilson called "the war to end all wars," Germany would suffer over 1,800,000 dead (over 30 times the number the United States lost in Vietnam) and over 4,000,000 wounded. Finally, as a reminder of the war, German society would be left with over 1,500,000 who were permanently disabled.

At home, daily life was hardly cheerful for those Germans who were spared the carnage on the battlefield. The success of the Royal Navy's blockade meant food-importing Germany was to run increasingly short of the most basic sources of nourishment as the hostilities continued. The lack of sufficient sustenance caused numerous premature deaths, particularly among the elderly, the invalid, and the very young. One German source estimates the British blockade led to as many as 763,000 fatalities.

As the food shortage grew, the Kaiser's government desperately searched for substitutes. Harnessing the scientific, and particularly chemical, expertise available, the German government experimented with a wide range of fake foods. Since fat was an enduring deficiency in the wartime diet, substitutes were attempted using rats, mice, hamsters and even cockroaches. For rather obvious cultural reasons, none of these were very successful as the average German palate revolted at the attempt to market "roach pate." As sausages were filled with sawdust, and beer transformed into an almost unrecognizable weak broth, some tried to be optimistic. The *Vossische Zeitung*, for instance, argued the food shortages were a disguised blessing since overeating caused baldness. Most Germans, however, found it difficult to agree with such optimism.

While the details may have varied from country to country, none of the major European combatants escaped devastating losses on the field of battle. Likewise, all suffered extreme deprivations at home. Meanwhile, the old class antagonism reasserted itself as many workers grew increasingly resentful of the way the upper classes were able to maintain their lifestyles while the average person fought to scrap by. Since many workers never really renounced their prewar radical beliefs, the inevitable war profiteering and the inequalities of warfare persuaded them that the war was little more than a capitalist struggle where, as Rosa Luxemburg put it, "profits rose and proletarians fell." After the Russian Revolution of 1917, resignation and hopelessness often changed into anger and energy as there seemed to be a simple solution. For many, the simple solution was revolution.

The Kaiser Goes, the Generals Remain

As the nation with one of the strongest left-wing traditions, it is not surprising that the torment of the war would ultimately produce an extreme reaction from the mass of the German populace. In early 1918, a general strike involving between 250,000 and 400,000 workers, swept Berlin and twenty-one other major urban areas. The strikers' demands were more than economic as they called for peace without annexations or indemnities. Further, they openly supported the Bolshevik People's Commissioner, Leon Trotsky's terms for peace with Soviet Russia. For workers to strike at defense plants during war time was certainly a sign of how much the antiwar sentiment had grown among the masses.

Although the strike was brutally crushed by military authorities, the situation continued to degenerate. Short of manpower at both the front and at home, the army had drafted thousands of the more militant strikers. This solved the problem for the moment, but ultimately accelerated the collapse of military morale—for drafted strikers spread their ideas among the already demoralized troops. By the October, General Erich von Ludendorff (1865–1937), Senior Quartermaster-General and Germany's virtual military dictator for the last two years of the war, confided his daily fear that his army on the western front would revolt and "flee across the Rhine and bring revolution to Germany."

This never happened because the spark that set Germany a flame came from an unlikely source: the Imperial German Navy. Having been humiliated earlier by the British, the German Navy had spent most of the war patrolling the coastal areas under the protection of shore batteries. With the end of the war clearly in sight, most sailors looked forward to peace and a safe return home. Some admirals, however, had other ideas.

On October 28, the Imperial German High Seas fleet began to assemble outside Wilhelmshaven Naval Station in the North Sea. The idea of surrendering the fleet to the soon-to-be victorious British was impossible for many in the naval establishment to accept. The leaders of the German Navy had resolved to send the entire High Seas fleet on one last attack against the superior British naval forces. Even though few admirals thought this last desperate gamble would succeed, or even change the course of the war, they wanted to, in the words of Admiral von Trotha, "go under with honor."

Once the sailors, many of whom now saluted one another with "Long Live Liebknecht" rather than "Long Live the Kaiser," learned of this plan, they were furious. When the first two ships, the *Thüringen* and the *Helgoland*, were ordered out to sea, the crews mutinied. All attempts at suppression failed as the thin veneer of discipline began to crack throughout the fleet. Soon, the Imperial standards were replaced by red flags and the fleet returned to port. This mutiny was the spark that would set Germany on fire. Workers throughout the coastal area rose up as news of the mutiny spread, often by sailors on their way home. By the end of the first week in November, Bremen, Hamburg, Lübeck and other smaller towns were in the hands of rebels. Throughout Germany, workers and soldiers councils—much like better known the Russian soviets—were organized.

On November 7, 1918, over 100,000 people in Munich occupied government buildings and seized all the strategic points in Bavaria's capital. The next day, they proclaimed the People's Republic of Bavaria. By now, all the major urban areas of Saxony, Baden, Hesse-

Darmstadt and Württemburg were in open revolt. The Kaiser, his generals (who were the real rulers by then), and their wealthy supporters were all but completely isolated and the military leaders were unsure if they could really rule Germany. On the morning of November 9, the Imperial Army unit commanders reported on the attitude of their troops towards the Kaiser and "Bolshevism." Their verdict was clear: their men would not fight to save the monarchy while their willingness to shed blood to stop the revolution was doubtful, at best. Thus, Kaiser Wilhelm II, ruler of Germany by grace of God, fled into exile in the Netherlands.

Aborted Revolution in Germany

As the Kaiser took the train toward Holland, workers and soldiers councils continued to spring up across Germany. These councils, or *räte* as they were known in German, resembled ever so much the soviets which had played a vital role in the Bolshevik-led revolution in Russia. In town after town, the power passed into the hands of ordinary citizens who most of all wanted peace but also some type of socialism. Factories were occupied, police disarmed and radicals chosen spontaneously to replace discredited officials. So for a historical moment it appeared as if Germany might follow the Russian model and move towards some type of socialist republic.

Fortunately for the large German industrialists and estate owners, this was not to be. Unlike Russia, there existed a powerful and intelligent force which would moderate the more revolutionary demands of the masses. That force was the conservatives within the Social Democratic Party which had earlier supported the war. With the fall of the Kaiser, Prince Max of Baden asked this group to form a new government. The brilliance of this move was clear to both the generals and the big bourgeoisie. They realized that only a group with popular support could derail the ever growing revolutionary movement. In addition, this new "socialist" government would find itself forced to sign the inescapable surrender treaty.

These people, in the words of SPD leader Friedrich Ebert (1871–

1925), "hated revolution like mortal sin." They set out to cool off the situation and establish a liberal republic. Wedded to the idea of parliamentary democracy and opposed to a situation of dual power, the SPD sent its supporters into the worker's and soldier's Councils in order to destroy them from within. With its sizable apparatus and experience, the SPD was successful in convincing many workers that socialism would be created, but in an orderly manner. Thus, in mid-December, SPD arguments about "democracy" and "order" convinced the first national *räte* congress to commit political suicide and call for elections to a national assembly.

Rather than follow in Kerensky's footsteps, Ebert, Philipp Scheidemann and their colleagues managed to do, or at the very least say, what was necessary to avoid completely alienating their working class base. Firstly, the Social Democrats knew the war had to be ended. Every day that the war continued was a day that the radicalization of the population would proceed. Therefore, the new government ended hostilities and began armistice negotiations. While militarists like Ludendorff would later cite this "stab in the back" as a reason for supporting Hitler, at the time they realized the war was hopelessly lost and had to be ended.

On the factory floor, the idea of worker's control of industry or some form of socialization was overwhelming popular. After all, many workers reasoned, why not bring down the war profiteers after they had accumulated so much wealth? To placate these revolutionary demands, the new "socialist" government set up a commission headed by the eminent Karl Kautsky to determine the exact procedures for nationalization of industry. Of course, by the time the commission was later disbanded, not a single workplace had been touched.

If the leaders of the Social Democrats had more faith in their supporters, they could have tried to use them to combat the smaller, but ever growing, revolutionary left led by Rosa Luxemburg and Karl Liebknecht. Ebert and his associates had, however, lost faith not only in a radical vision of socialism, but even in their own followers. Therefore, they entered into an unlikely alliance which was, according to many historians, to doom the new German republic. Approached by General Wilhelm Gröner who had the blessing of Field Marshal Paul von Hindenburg (1847–1934), Friedrich Ebert agreed to support the restoration of the authority of the army. In return for a pledge not to purge, or in any way interfere with the military, the army promised to support the new government in "fighting Bolshevism."

A situation ensued where the government would leave all the levers of power—military, judicial, financial—in the same hands they had been under the Kaiser. As a result, the most important positions in German society outside of the formal governmental structure would be overwhelmingly anti-democratic and often monarchist. As for their promise to support the government, the army honored its word only as it applied to the left, for when Hitler came to prominence it quickly reached an accommodation with fascism. The tragic irony is that the Social Democrats' commitment to order led them to prop up many old institutions and individuals who would later allow the Nazi dictatorship to be established.

Suppression of the Revolutionary Left

In a Germany which was in a state of virtually constant flux, the possibility of the revolutionary left recouping its early losses to the moderate Social Democrats remained a possibility in late 1918 and 1919. After all, the war's end did little to immediately improve the living standard of workers. Real wages had dropped to little more than 70 percent of their prewar level while unemployment skyrocketed: almost doubling from the start of December 1918 to January 1919. Many continued to live on the brink of starvation as the Allied blockade was not lifted until July 12, 1919.

The revolutionary left—including the Spartakusbund, the Bremen Left Radicals, and other regional groupings—had coalesced into the German Communist Party (KPD) at the end of 1918. Blessed with a skillful leadership including Luxemburg, Liebknecht, Zetkin, and Mehring, this group had great potential for rapid growth among radicalized urban workers. For example, the KPD seemed likely to win over the more radical members of the Independent Social Democratic Party (which it later did). In time, the KPD leadership thought that the mass of workers would be convinced of the futility of supporting the reformism of the Social Democrats.

Time was, however, something the German Communists never really had. Soon after their founding party congress in January 1919, street fighting broke out in Berlin when the government dismissed that city's popular (and radical) police chief. Although the KPD leadership knew an uprising was tragically premature, they refused to abandon the radical workers. Seizing on this incident, the Social Democrats sent in troops (many of them private, proto-fascist *Freikorps*) who brutally suppressed the Berlin radicals. Among the numerous victims of this repression were many working women (it would be a mistake to think of this rebellion as an exclusively male affair.) Within a few days, hundreds, if not thousands, of workers had paid for their beliefs with their lives.

Nor were the killings to be a result of the emotions unleashed just during the heat of battle. The two most renowned KPD leaders, Rosa Luxemburg and Karl Liebknecht, were arrested and ruthlessly murdered on January 15. Both had expected imprisonment as in the Kaiser's day, neither could imagine they would be killed under a "socialist"-led republic. The assassins when later tried received a light jail term, which they never served because they almost immediately were allowed to escape from prison.

The suppression of radical Berlin and the murder of Luxemburg and Liebknecht were the beginning of a pattern in the new republic. Any rebellion or even hint of disorder from the left was met with fierce repression while even the most cold-blooded murder committed by the right was seldom punished by a judicial system composed of reactionary monarchists. In the months that followed Berlin's "January Days," radical workers were set upon throughout urban Germany. Kurt Eisner, a leader of Bavaria's Independent Social Democrats, was murdered in broad daylight on the steps of the regional parliament building by a monarchist officer on February 21.

In April, a Soviet Republic was proclaimed in Bavaria, mainly in the capital of Munich. Although the original attempt, led by anarchists and an odd assortment of poets, was opposed by the Communists and their Munich leader Eugene Leviné (1883–1919), as in Berlin, the KPD was drawn into the struggle after a few weeks. After the Soviet was crushed in May, Leviné was condemned to death for high treason although the court acknowledged that the Soviet Republic was proclaimed "despite Leviné's opposition." Before sentence was pronounced, the leader of the Bavarian KPD addressed the court noting that the Soviet was started by noncommunists who eventually fled while "we Communists are stood up against the wall." Grimly aware of his fate, yet still defiant, Leviné said, "we Communists are all dead men on leave."

March of the following year, 1920, saw the Kapp Putsch, an attempted monarchical coup defeated, not by the army who had promised to defend the government, but by a general strike which caused this movement to fizzle out. This attempt to overthrow the government arose because the government felt forced to start dissolving *Freikorps* units in order to comply with the Allied demand that the military not exceed 100,000. This episode well illustrated the lack of loyalty many officers and soldiers felt to the new government.

Later the same month, radical workers in the Ruhr mining districts rose up and occupied their mines only to be crushed by the army. By 1921, the revolutionary left in Germany was exhausted and bleeding. Any possibility for fundamental social change beyond the limits of now-moderate Social Democracy was not immediately on the agenda. There would be other chances, most notably during the year 1923, but reformism had triumphed temporarily. More ominously, the forerunners of fascism were active in suppressing the revolutionary left while biding time until they would be able to destroy the Weimar Republic. A confused mixture of old monarchists and disoriented veterans, these far right elements would make little distinction between democratic government and "godless communism." These soon-to-be fascists flooded Germany with the most vile anti-Semitic publications while also playing on male fears by claiming socialism would mean "free love" and an end to all family life.

Collapse of the Hapsburg Monarchy

In the aftermath of the Revolutions of 1848, the Austrian Empire had been transformed into a "dual monarchy" known as Austria-Hungary which appeared by 1867. Although Imperial Germany had suffered during the First World War, it was not much different for the Empire to the southeast. By the end of the fighting, Austria-Hungary had suffered 1,200,000 dead and over 3,600,000 wounded. By 1918 as the armies increasingly disintegrated, the urban areas, particularly the great industrial center of Vienna, became more openly rebellious. By fall, the once mighty Empire seemed to be competing with Imperial Germany to see which could collapse first. Finally on November 11, 1918, Kaiser Karl abdicated as his erstwhile empire broke into its constituent ethnic parts. Austria and Hungary were the most economically developed and politically radical of the new nations created. An Austrian Republic was proclaimed with fewer than 8,000,000 inhabitants while a Hungarian Republic was established with only slightly more citizens.

Austro-Marxism and Revolutionary Vienna

Unlike the German Social Democrats whose apparatus remained under the control of moderates, the Austrian Social Democratic Party (SPÖ) had moved leftward during the war. Old reformist leaders lost influence as younger and, at least theoretically, more radical leaders came to fore. Among them was Friedrich Adler who was not only the son of one of the party's most prominent leaders but also extremely popular for assassinating the Austrian Prime Minister as a protest against the war. Another notable leader to emerge was Otto Bauer (1882–1938) who was a Marxist theoretician of considerable power and a leading contributor to a theoretical school of thought known as Austro-Marxism.

Alongside people such as these who were trusted and who gave the appearances of being sincere revolutionaries, German SPD leaders like Ebert and Scheidemann appeared positively pale by comparison. Austro-Marxists were unique not in their criticism of reformism but that they sought to develop a revolutionary theory apart from—if not hostile to—Bolshevism. At least up to their suppression by Hitler, this tendency represented an alternative to both the old Social Democracy and Russia's form of Communism.

This change in the SPÖ was in response to the radicalization of their rank and file members. In addition, the impact of the Russian Revolution was propagated by many returning prisoners of war, trained by the Bolsheviks. Although the tone of Austrian Social Democracy had become revolutionary, its actions were not. This party was more of the centrist than revolutionary type. Although conditions in Austria were perhaps more ripe for revolution than almost anywhere else, the Austrian Social Democratic leadership always found excuses to avoid pushing the struggle toward revolution. The party did accomplish social and economic reforms like the eight hour day and quality public housing (unlike that too often found in the United States today).

When they talked about pushing the revolution forward, the party's leadership discovered insurmountable obstacles. First, the SPÖ claimed to be prisoners of the victorious western nations who, in Bauer's words, "could cut off supplies of food and coal, thus starving us out, occupy our territory with its troops, or expose us to the attacks of neighboring states. Thus, the power of the victors set very definite limits upon the proletarian revolution in Austria." Further, Austrian Social Democrats pointed to the conservatism of the food producing provinces of Tyrol and Voralberg, which might secede and, thus, starve out Vienna. In fact, concerted action may well have carried the day for revolutionary change given the overwhelming radical mood among Austria's proletariat. Yet the possibility of foreign intervention or civil war cannot be dismissed easily. Ultimately, it remains sheer speculation whether or not revolution was possible in Austria.

Nevertheless, when it came to the question of military power, the Austrian socialists were not to make the same mistake their German colleagues had. They organized a truly republican army made up of working class elements of the old imperial army. Both soldiers' councils and radical Red Guard units were incorporated into this unique structure. In fact, one of its major battalions was heavily communist. Further, the council or *räte* movement was turned into an instrument of "proletarian democracy," which the SPÖ dominated rather than merely dismissed as Ebert's people had done. While in Germany, the mainstream SPD had demobilized the workers; in Austria, the SPÖ keep the working class actively involved.

Thus, the relatively weak Austrian Communist Party (KPÖ) was in an untenable position. They drew support mainly from Vienna's unemployed, war invalids, and returning prisoners of war radicalized in Russia. Unlike the KPD, the Austrian Communists found themselves isolated from those they sought to lead since most workers sincerely believed the SPÖ was building socialism. When the Communists took action in the spring of 1919, it was, at best, ill advised, at worst, stupid. The KPÖ's lack of mass support was demonstrated convincingly on July 21 when a Comintern-sponsored call for a general strike in support of the Hungarian Soviet Republic fell on deaf ears.

Soviet Republic in Hungary

If conditions favored a more revolutionary course in Austria which was not taken, less favorable conditions in Hungary failed to preclude a revolutionary experiment. The collapse of the old regime had more or less followed the pattern set in Germany and Austria. By 1917, the losses on the battlefield united with political repression and economic inequality at home to produce a wave of popular unrest. During the last two years of the war a series of bitter industrial conflicts took place which climaxed in a general strike. The strike itself, which began in Budapest and spread throughout Hungary, occurred in June 1918.

On the last day of October 1918, workers, soldiers, and young people seized the major strategic points and public buildings in Budapest. In response, the King of Hungary appointed a new liberal Prime Minister who established a coalition government that included the Hungarian Social Democrats. This new bourgeois democratic government, the first independent Hungarian government to exist since 1848, had every hope that the victorious Allies would assist them in constructing a liberal republic. Yet, the western powers looked upon the new leaders in Budapest as little more than a continuation of the old Dual Monarchy and offered neither concessions nor help.

Hungarian Social Democracy rapidly lost support among its working class base since participation in the new regime resulted in little improvement as far as the average proletarian could discern. The Socialists were further undercut by the activities of the Communist Party, organized in November under the leadership of Béla Kun (1886–1939). Most prominent in the new party were Hungarians who had been converted to Bolshevism while POWS in Russia. In addition to former prisoners, the party drew heavily from the unemployed, disgruntled soldiers and various groups within the urban working class of Budapest along with an assortment of radical intellectuals. Calling for immediate radical changes, the Hungarian Communists worked for a second Bolshevik-style revolution. By February 1919, the new liberal government rounded-up the bulk of the Communist leadership.

In the rapidly changing sentiments of the time, this government crackdown was initially supported by broad sections of the urban population, many of whom nonetheless switched their sympathies to the Communist within a matter of only a few weeks. By March, significant numbers of workers from the larger Budapest factories were vigorously demanding the release of the Communist leaders. This internal dissent became more critical because of the utter failure of the bourgeois democratic government in the field of foreign affairs. The bulk of Hungary's territory was under foreign military occupation by the western Allies. When the western victors decided to give Transylvania to Romania, despite impassioned pleas from Budapest, the middle-class government could no longer govern and the Prime Minister resigned.

Into this power vacuum stepped the Hungarian left. On 21, March

1919, the Hungarian Social Democrats and Communists agreed to take power jointly while Hungary was declared a council republic and an ally of Soviet Russia. Incredibly, this new government was constructed with almost no internal opposition. Even those groups, such as the large landowners and bourgeoisie, which would appear to have the most to lose under such a regime, offered no resistance. One reason for this unusual reaction was the hope shared by the majority of Hungarians that the new government might be able to prevent further occupation of Hungarian territory, if not prevent the annexation of areas inhabited by Hungarians temporarily under foreign rule.

Collapse of the Soviet Government in Hungary

This "honeymoon" was short lived as Béla Kun and his radical government were to have little under a month of peace. In April, the month following Béla Kun's rise to power in Budapest, Hungary was set upon by first the Romanian and then the Czechoslovak armies. Whereas opposition to the new radical government was widely trumpeted as the reason for their intervention, there is little doubt the desire for territorial expansion was a major motivation for both invading armies. To defend besieged Hungary, the Soviet government needed to mobilize the population.

Although fairly effective in rallying workers in Budapest, the peasantry remained relatively impervious to the call to arms. This resulted from a major tactical error on the part of the left-wing administration, which had nationalized rather than redistributed the lands confiscated from the large feudal estates. Matters worsened rapidly with the repressive actions which alienated not only the peasantry but also the middle class and noncommunist intellectuals who otherwise might have rallied to the cause of national self-defense. Within two months of its formation, the new government had squandered most of the good will it had acquired upon seizing power.

By May, the superior power of the external invaders had effectively broken the will of the only partially established red army. By then, the fall of the Hungarian Soviet Republic was only a matter of time. When the Romanian army entered Budapest in the early days of

August, there was little support remaining for the Soviet experiment even among Budapest's industrial working class. Rather than build the basis for liberation, Béla Kun had instead paved the way for a right-wing authoritarian government which took power on August 6, 1919. This new regime would be notable for anti-Semitism and political repression, not to mention its later alliance with Hitler's Germany. As Hungarian radicals either fled, were jailed or slain, this dictatorship would last a quarter of a century when it was finally overthrown at the end of the Second World War.

Anti-Semitism and Revolutionary Movements

Rather than withering away as an outmoded and unscientific ideology as socialists like Bebel and Engels had thought, anti-Semitism was to acquire new strength during the pandemonium that followed World War I. Not only were Trotsky and many other highly visible Bolshevik leaders of Jewish origin, a significant number of leading revolutionaries in other nations, particularly Germany, Austria, and Hungary were also Jewish. The reality that the vast bulk of Jews were as patriotic as anyone else escaped most anti-Semites. (In fact, German Jews won a higher proportion of military decorations than any other group.)

Instead, the prominence of radicals like Rosa Luxemburg in Berlin, Eugene Leviné in Munich, or Otto Bauer in Vienna was cited as "proof" that socialism was a Jewish plot. When subject to reason, such claims were, of course, ridiculous. Sadly, the extreme right never allowed facts to cloud its vision of a "Jewish conspiracy." For their part, revolutionaries, even those from a Jewish background, seldom found anti-Semitism worthy of a serious response, and allowed many ludicrous arguments to go unanswered. Thus, anti-Semitism became a powerful weapon for mobilizing conservative support against revolutionary movements or even more moderate socialist parties, as well as Jewish citizens.

Ironically, the anti-Semites had largely themselves to blame for the high proportion of Jews involved in Socialist or Communist movements. True, most Jews lived in urban areas where the population of whatever religious background was more likely to support the left. Still, it was the anti-Semitism of most non-socialist parties which forced many European Jews to support the left. This in turn supplied the right with the impressionistic evidence they used to build their conspiracy theories. In Austria, after the First World War, some 75 percent of Jewish citizens usually voted for the Socialists but given the virulent anti-Semitism of the alternatives, this should come as little surprise. Likewise the large number of Jewish leaders in left-wing movements was largely the result of Jews being unwelcome, if not prohibited from leadership positions, and sometimes even membership, in other organizations.

The First World War's Impact on Italy

Thus far, the revolutionary upheaval has been examined only in those defeated nations in which popular frustration combined with the ignominy of military loss worked to sweep away those previously in power. It was not, however, only the "losers" who were subject to revolutionary upheavals. In Northern Italy, particularly the cities of Turin, Milan, and Genoa, the end of the war marked the start of a two year long period of intense class struggle. During 1919 and 1920, the years of the "biennio rosso," industrial workers fought against their employers by utilizing radical and often innovative methods of struggle including factory occupations and the establishment of worker's councils, which were seen by many as the prototype of a new society.

During the First World War, life was difficult at best for the average Italian industrial worker who was forced to labor long hours for an uncertain supply of food and consumer goods. For those either in the army or without industrial employment, life was even harsher. The overwhelming peasant army contrasted their harsh and often brief lives with those still living at home. Although Italy had entered World War I against Austria-Hungary only in 1915, not even declaring war on Germany until August 28, 1916, the losses were nonetheless devastating. By the time of the armistice, Italy had lost 460,000 and 947,000 had been wounded (over four times the losses of the United States). While morale in the Italian armed forces was never as bad as that in pre-revolutionary Russia or even France, by 1917 it was quite low. In the summer of 1917, for instance, an entire regiment mutinied.

Food shortages plagued the Italians throughout the war. There is evidence that some peasants hoped for a quick Austrian victory just so the war would end. Meanwhile, women in Naples were heard to say "with the Germans at least we would have bread." In August 1917 in Turin, rioting provoked by bread shortages grew into a prolonged proletarian insurrection which lasted over four days. Working class women led this revolt when bakers said they were out of bread yet continued to produce expensive sweet rolls for the rich. Since civilian urban discontent never successfully linked up with the largely peasant army, events in Italy would be far different from those in Russia or Germany. Still, by the war's conclusion, pent-up frustration would explode in a variety of dramatic ways. The Italian Socialist Party (PSI) had never supported the war and had become, verbally, more revolutionary. To some contemporary observers, Italy appeared on the brink of revolt by the end of 1918.

The Biennio Rosso in Northern Italy

Perhaps nowhere were these developments more striking than in Turin, a city dominated by the massive concentrated industrial power of Fiat. The ever increasing demands of the wartime economy had forced Fiat to expand its work force from 3,500 in April 1915 to over 40,000 by the conflict's conclusion. This expansion was more than quantitative since the new workers were recruited from non-traditional groups such as women, farm workers, unskilled adolescents, and even immigrants forcibly removed from Italian overseas colonies. Nor was this increase in new workers unique to Fiat. By 1916, the city of Turin had grown by 22 percent by adding almost 100,000 inhabitants over its 1911 population.

This heterogeneous proletariat labored under a system far different from the prewar economy, which had relied on skilled workers. During the First World War, the Italian working class was subject to a regimentation which attempted to substitute new industrial processes for the previous reliance on a skilled labor force. The newly proletarianized laborers at Fiat had little time to reflect upon what must have been a dramatic change in lifestyle. Although the Italian government's official work week was supposed to be seventy hours, overtime in Turin's Fiat plants caused the average week to grow to seventy-five plus hours while real wages declined.

Within the Fiat plants, a powerful series of factory councils, often likened to soviets, grew up during the war. The factory council was much different from the traditional trade union because every worker in the plant was entitled to participate in it, regardless of political or union affiliation. Moreover, the councils increasingly saw themselves as the models for a new democratically controlled economy rather than as a bargaining tool with capital. These potentially revolutionary organizations were to be instrumental in September 1920 when workers seized the factories and declared their intention to run the plants. Had these uprisings, which spread throughout the industrial areas of the North, been extended by the PSI to the entire country, a revolutionary transformation might have been possible. At a minimum, there might have been some degree of democratization in a country where the king still had significant power and women still could not vote. Instead, there was little attempt to coordinate actions between the urban areas, mobilize the peasantry, or subvert the armed forces. Thus quarantined, the revolutionary movement failed.

The failure of what appeared to be a promising moment for drastic social change, which might have preempted Mussolini's fascist movement, was to have grave consequences. Why then was so little effort made to generalize a movement which offered a vision of democratic grass roots control of society? First, the isolation of urban workers from the large number of rural Italians must be remembered. Those who lived in rural areas were little touched by socialist agitation. Further, even within the urban working class, the strength of the reformist Confederation of Labor (CGL) continued to be significant for the CGL had almost 2,000,000 members to, at best, the 200,000 in the PSI.

Finally, the inertia of the Italian Socialist Party must be credited with undermining what potential the red years of 1919–1920 might have possessed. The PSI was wedded to a more or less deterministic brand of Marxism which saw history as leading to their inevitable victory and left little room for innovation or a rapid change in tactics. The leaders of Italian Socialism were pleased with the struggles in the North, but they did little to maximize impact of the uprisings. Presented with a genuine proletarian movement of tremendous power, the PSI did nothing. Neither was an attempt made to win the peasantry over to a revolutionary perspective nor did the Socialists woo disgruntled ex-soldiers. "We, as Marxists," Serrati noted in the PSI's defense in October 1919, "interpret history. We do not make it." Neither employers nor fascists took such a passive view. By 1921, the worker's movement was in retreat, reeling from an industrial crisis that prompted massively layoffs and wage cuts. The following year, 1922, Mussolini would seize power and proceed to construct a totalitarian fascist regime.

Revolutionary Dissent in France

The battlefields on the western front took place largely on French soil which was watered with the blood of an immense number of French soldiers. Of the male population between the ages of twenty and thirty-two as of 1914, over half died during the war. Not only did 1,385,000 French citizens die, an additional 700,000 men were crippled while almost 2,400,000 were wounded. One must also add to the price in human life, the immense cost in property destruction which included 300,000 ruined houses and 20,000 devastated factories and workshops.

These cold statistics might have been even greater if the French high command had its way and had been able to continue with the human wave assaults so popular among all the generals of the warring armies. In April 1917, however, many French soldiers took matters into their own hands. On the 29th of that month, a battalion of the 18th regiment which had lost two-thirds of its men in a recent assault, refused orders to return to the line. With the swift arrest and execution of the leaders of this soldiers' strike, the French military thought there would be no more insurrection. Instead, the mutiny spread to 110 units within six weeks.

Eating wretched food and receiving inadequate medical attention, many French troops despised the army staff officers who disdained from even soling their uniforms. Further, many soldiers were upset that they did not receive regular leave from the front, while most of all, they felt their lives were being capriciously tossed away in pointless assaults against the German trenches. By June, the government was informed that there were only two completely reliable divisions between Paris and the enemy lines.

Suppression of the Mutiny

As the mutiny progressed, it became tinged with the red hue of social revolution. Antiwar propaganda and the example of the Russian Revolution combined with preexisting radical sentiments among many troops produced a scene which certainly frightened official Paris. The red flag appeared among many of the rebellious troops while mutineers sang the socialist song "The Internationale" and called for international solidarity. Regiments formed councils, much like the Russian soviets, and elected their leaders while attacking officers who attempted to restore discipline.

To cope with this dire situation, the army turned to General Henri-Philippe Pétain (1856–1951) who was known as the "hero of Verdun." Pétain attacked the mutiny with a blend of concessions and brutality in a manner that would foreshadow his role as Hitler's puppet ruler in the Southern French Vichy government during World War II. To restore morale, all regimental cooks were given cooking lessons while a regular leave policy was instituted. Not all of Pétain's responses were so benign. Officers were ordered to do whatever was necessary to restore discipline and rumors have persisted of whole units marched into isolated areas and blown to pieces by their own artillery.

While the exact number of executions will never be known, the official French figure of twenty-three is laughable, even if one British estimate of 30,000 appears somewhat exaggerated. Yet, even government records admit that over 23,000 soldiers were tried and sentenced while, of course, this does not include all those "dealt with" in the field. In any event, it is certain that a massive number of French soldiers paid for the mutiny with their lives or least their liberty. All the same, the revolt was not without impact, for Pétain promised that there would be no more massive attacks, and he did limit his assaults to a small number of troops supported by massive amounts of covering artillery fire.

Urban Unrest

Not only was the French army mutiny a threat to the war effort, it potentially threatened the entire social structure. This is particularly so as there existed serious unrest within the civilian working class during the same period. In May 1917, while the mutiny was at the peak of its activity, demonstrations broke out in Paris and other large urban areas that witnessed huge crowds waving red flags as they cried, "Down with the war." Key industrial unions, like the metal workers, called for action against this "capitalist war."

Yet, the government was able to weather this storm of protest which turned out to be stronger on rhetoric than actual rebellion. By a combination of repression and promises, any actual threat to the social order was avoided. Further, the swift destruction of the army mutiny had precluded the possibility of an alliance between disgruntled soldiers and radical workers. Still, sections of the population clearly were willing to consider a "Russian solution" to the problems the war caused. Within the organized left, the bulk of the old socialist SFIO became more radical and established the Parti Communiste Français (PCF).

The Easter Rebellion in Ireland

When put beside the turmoil which beset most of Europe during 1917–1921, Great Britain would at first appear to be an island of social stability. British difficulties with revolutionaries at home seemed mild in comparison with those of the nation's continental neighbors. However, the "Irish Question" must be taken into account. Occupying Ireland for centuries, English landowners and industrialists had long gazed upon the native Irish population as a rowdy and amusing group of primitives. The Irish, however, were not overly fond of the English. Throughout the nineteenth century, Irish nationalism had been growing steadily and was kept at bay only by a combination of repression and concessions. By the twentieth century, a small but vital Irish labor movement had developed under a clearly radical leadership which promoted not only national independence but also socialism.

Foremost in this regard was James Connolly (1868–1916) who was the first major Marxist trade union leader in Ireland. In 1896, soon after his arrival in Dublin, Connolly helped found the Irish Socialist Republican Party which demanded an Irish Socialist Republic based on public ownership of land, instruments of production, distribution, and exchange. The following year he founded a newspaper entitled *Workers' Republic* in addition to writing *Erin's Hope* which argued for socialism based on the Irish clan tradition of common ownership of the land, a thesis more fully developed in *Labour in Irish History*.

In 1903, Connolly made what he was to call the biggest mistake of his life. He moved to the United States. Until 1910, he lived in New York City isolated from the struggle at home. Yet, he became an organizer for the Socialist Party of America as well as the Industrial Workers of the World (IWW). While in the United States, Connolly was influenced by syndicalism and became a pioneer in the theory of worker's control of industry.

Returning to Ireland in July 1910, Connolly immersed himself in national politics. By 1912 at Clonmel, he and James Larkin (1876–1947) founded the Irish Labour Party with the backing of the Irish Trade

Union Congress. He was Larkin's chief assistant in organizing the Irish National Transport and General Workers' Union, which conducted sympathy strikes in support of other labor disputes. In 1913, the Dublin industrialists instituted a lockout against members of the union and brutally suppressed the resulting labor demonstrations.

At that time, Connolly became commander of an irregular Irish Citizen Army that was to protect workers from police assault. With the outbreak of World War I, he replaced Larkin, who was visiting America, as head of the union. Horrified at the disintegration of the European socialist movement and maintaining that peace could be assured only through the collapse of the capitalist system, Connolly pledged the Irish labor movement to an antiwar position. He believed that only a working class uprising could bring the war to a halt. At the same time, he felt that such an uprising could bring about the national liberation of Ireland.

When plans for a rebellion became known to the British authorities, Connolly decisively chose to act at once. Known to history as the Easter Rising, the revolt began on April 24, 1916 in Dublin. Although he knew there was almost no hope of success, Connolly felt honor bound to make some attempt to spark a revolution.

On Easter Monday the revolutionaries seized the Dublin General Post Office where an Irish republic was proclaimed. The English government's response was fierce. Before the unconditional surrender on April 29, over 1,300 people had been killed or wounded and 179 buildings in central Dublin had been destroyed. After the uprising had been squashed with brutal ruthlessness, ninety rebels were tried and condemned to death by secret court martial.

Despite world wide pleas on his behalf, on May 12, James Connolly, twice wounded and suffering from gangrene, was placed on a stretcher and carried to a place of execution. Once there, he was bound to a chair and shot by a firing squad. While remembered today as most primarily a nationalist, Connolly clearly saw the national question as intertwined with the struggle for a socialist society. Of course, Connolly was only one of several Irish activists involved in planning the Easter Uprising, and his socialist politics differed from those of these Irish Nationalists.

Rebellious Britain, 1918–1919

Nor were Britain's problems exclusively limited to Ireland. Much like France, Great Britain had taken terrible losses on the battlefield while endeavoring to overcome German steel with British flesh and spirit. With almost a million dead and over two million wounded, Britain's causalities were greater than those of the United States, Italy, and the Ottoman Empire combined. Whatever spirit of patriotism had inspired men onward into combat in the first months of the war was gone by 1917. That year, a visitor to the British base camp in France wrote of a strange expression on the faces of the soldiers. The look of the troops was not one of despair or terror. Rather, it was a "blindfold look, and without expression, like a dead rabbit's."

This look was reflected in increasing insubordination and, by 1919, actual strikes among the armed forces in both France and Egypt. At home, members of the working class had long grown resentful at the continuing sacrifices being asked of them by those above who sacrificed little. As a result, during the winter of 1918–1919, radical socialist ideas gained ground in Great Britain's cities notably on the "red Clyde" where workers were in an almost openly revolutionary mood. Within the military, officers had simply lost the ability to command in many units. Moreover, many of the strikes in the armed forces were a result of anger over the demobilization plans.

Thus, during the cold months after the end of the war, it appeared that the stability of British society was in doubt. Yet, these two parallel rebellious trends never linked up largely because the domestic left gave little thought to the condition of the armed forces. This omission precluded the growth of what might have been a very serious revolutionary opposition to the status quo in Great Britain. Not until the General Strike of 1926 would the powerful again actually sleep uneasy because of labor rebellion.

Ebbing of the Revolutionary Tide

By the end of 1921, it was becoming apparent that the old order had weathered the worst of the storm unleashed by World War I. In retrospect, this upheaval centered mainly on Russia because the old Czarist system had been relegated to the "dust bin of history" while the self-proclaimed socialist government of the Bolsheviks was in place in Moscow. Further, the war had accelerated the collapse of the Ottoman Empire and Austria-Hungary while the Kaiser's Germany was now a liberal republic. Other European states had witnessed outbreaks of rebellion which shook the confidence of their elites. The map of the European continent was profoundly redrawn. The Austro-Hungarian Empire was broken into pieces—Austria, Hungary, Czechoslovakia, and others—while the Ottoman Empire died and gave birth to modern Turkey. Poland reappeared as an independent nation for the first time in generations. Not only Germany's colonial possessions but also the Ottoman Empire's holdings in the Arab world passed over to the influence or control of the Allies.

Still, with the exception of Russia, the revolutionaries had ultimately failed in achieving their most important goals. Even those countries which had undergone a profound political transformation were still firmly, in some cases more firmly, in the hands of the capitalists. Of course, there were to be further upheavals particularly in Germany in 1923, but the tide of revolution which appeared ready to sweep Europe in 1917 had receded. Karl Liebknecht may have proclaimed the Socialist Republic in Germany, but it had never come to pass. Béla Kun's experiment in Hungary had been drowned in blood. What seemed like revolution in North Italy proved to be a crisis for—but not the end of—the status quo. Numerous nations had seen groups with as grand revolutionary hopes as these without even as many possibilities. Future revolutionary movements would have the twin added burdens of fascism in the west and Stalinism from the east. It remains now to consider why the revolution movement failed while recognizing what these efforts achieved.

Conclusion: The Significance of the Revolutionary Left in Europe

People "make their own history," Karl Marx once observed, "but not in conditions of their choosing." In many ways, this could well serve as an epitaph for Europe's revolutionaries in the half century between the Paris Commune of 1871 and the post-World War I failure of the radical left which was evident by 1921. Therefore, this is an appropriate year to end this examination as the years that followed were in many ways—fascism, the rise of the United States, Stalinism—fundamentally different. Their dreams, hopes and actions were fixed on a new world they would never see except for fleeting moments such as the Commune in Paris or the revolution in Russia.

Reasons for Revolutionary Failures

While the actions of the revolutionary left helped make history, the conditions were such that their failures were all too common while victories remained rare and momentary. Why did "the revolution" fail in Europe? This is not an easy question to answer, and numerous different interpretations have been given. With the advantage of hindsight, it is possible to note some circumstances which troubled the radical dream.

Persistence of the European Peasantry

Firstly, most of the revolutionaries discussed in this work were wedded to urban life. They had little interest and often less sympathy for what Marx called, "the idiocy of rural life." In return, the European peasantry was indifferent, if not usually hostile, to social movements or ideologies emanating from the city. An anecdote told by an Italian Marxist of talking with troops brought from the countryside into Turin to break a strike illustrates the vast gap between the two portions of popular society. When asked why they were there, a soldier answered they were going to "shoot the gentlemen who are on strike." Shocked, the socialist countered, "the strikers are only poor workers." At once, another soldier said "they wear shoes, so they must be gentlemen."

This fissure was not unbridgeable as the early support the Bolsheviks received from the land hungry peasants proved. Still, the rural population, even many of its most desperately poor elements, was fixated on the idea of land ownership. Not only did this desire tend to conflict with the prevailing revolutionary belief in large-scale collective agriculture, it also helped produce a type of petty-bourgeois mentality wedded to the idea of private property that led many rural citizens to identify with the far richer capitalists instead of with the urban workers. All the same, the bulk of the rural populace was far from well off, and an alliance with radicals of the urban centers was not out of the question.

Most revolutionaries dealt with this complex situation mainly by ignoring the problem. They regarded the peasantry as an economically doomed class, which would be destroyed by the laws of capitalist development. Abstractly, they may have been right. The problem, however, was that by the late nineteenth century governments throughout Europe began to prop up the farm population through various supports and subsidies. Had governments left their farmers to the tender mercies of the market, many more peasant families would have been forced from the land as the machinery necessary to compete successfully grew in cost.

Europe's governments preserved the peasantry precisely to prevent further proletarianization and the corresponding radicalization which typically followed. "We must prevent our loyal 'white' peasants," one German official noted, "from moving to cities where they become 'red.'" The inability of most of the left to realize the persistence of the peasantry and adjust their strategy accordingly helped pave the road to disaster.

Anti-Semitism and Racism

Likewise, the body of European "reds" failed to comprehend the continuing appeal of anti-Semitism and racism. Firm supporters of rationality, revolutionary leaders were convinced that reason would eventually strike down such unscientific beliefs. Few understood that prejudice's irrational appeal was such that facts alone were not a sufficient antidote. After all, racism was based on theories which depended not on reason, but on emotion. To argue, as Engels did in 1890, that anti-Semitism was "nothing but a reaction of declining medieval social strata against modern society" was to miss the point. As the twentieth century proved all too graphically, bigotry persisted and could be utilized by demagogues to motivate people to act, even against their own best interests. Given the large number of radicals of Jewish origin, anti-Semitism was a club which conservatives used to beat the left. Had revolutionaries better confronted anti-Semitism, it might have been diminished, but, again, their belief in science and reason subverted their potential effectiveness by causing a fatal underestimation of the power of hate.

The Troublesome Problem of Religion

Another example of the "dead hand of tradition" balancing the scales of history against the left was the question of religion. Revolutionaries were always attacked as irreligious atheists, a charge which was certainly true in numerous cases. Socialism was often seen as a substitute for religion, particularly in the sense that radicals would claim they were struggling for a society based on the very same values Christianity espoused but refused to practice. In fact, for countless Europeans, radical social movements were a substitute for religion. Witness Leon Trotsky, who when asked his religion, replied "I am a socialist." To many, therefore, radical social transformation was often seen as being counterposed to religious institutions, if not beliefs.

Bourgeois theories such as those which espoused the wonders of the free market were hardly listened to by most Europeans, save those of the upper classes. What did continue to hold the common people's attention, to varying degrees, was religion, particularly Christianity. Radicals realized that religion was "the heart of a heartless world" as Marx put it, but they felt compelled to reject its organized versions as institutions which sought to hold back human progress. Although revolutionaries sometimes appealed directly to the faithful over the heads of their hierarchy, as Rosa Luxemburg did in her *Socialism and the Churches*, too often radicals clung to the formula "religion is a private matter" and felt content to leave the subject stand there. The interminable and often vicious attacks upon the left from most religious institutions only hardened the revolutionary belief in the reactionary nature of faith. In the final analysis, nothing was able to completely shake some individuals' belief in religion. After all, as one socialist lamented, "we can only offer an end to hunger, churches offer everlasting life."

Sexuality and the Woman Question

Another area where tradition conspired with prejudice to weaken the revolutionary movement can be found in questions of gender and family relations. Radicals were constantly being accused of promoting immorality, wanting to "socialize women" and destroy the family. By putting forth the radical notion that women were human beings, the left found itself the target of all those threatened by the changing social structure of Europe. These changes, however, were the result of industrial capitalism and owed little to radical agitation. Yet this fact made little difference to those men who saw their traditional dominance called into question.

Many of the more immediate demands which radical movements made, such as giving women the vote, may seem tame today. Nonetheless, by challenging the accepted dogma of female inferiority, the left brought the wrath of many males (and some females content with their limitations) upon itself. Like religion, most radicals saw sexuality as a private matter. This led a number of revolutionaries to argue that people should be free to live as they saw fit, even if this included homosexual activity. This was hardly the sort of opinion which played well among the sexually insecure or the conservative.

Growth of Colonialism and Nationalism

Colonialism and its companion, racism against people of color, were to become a powerful weapon against the revolutionary left. By providing European workers with advantages, real or imagined, colonialism helped blunt the militant spirit of sections of the laboring population. Many believed that colonialism helped labor in the "mother country," and it certainly inspired nationalism as opposed to internationalism among many workers. This was one of the most important blessings of imperialism as some powerful capitalists even contended capitalism could not survive without empire. Thus, colonialism "is a bread and butter question," in the words of Cecil Rhodes, "If you want to avoid civil war, you must become imperialists."

A related difficulty which undermined the radical left was not just the tenacity, but the frequent growth of nationalist sentiment. The failure of the left to remain true to professed internationalist principles when confronted with the outbreak of the First World War epitomizes this dilemma. While the underlying causes for war had been discussed for decades and peace resolutions dutifully passed at radical gatherings (notably those of the Socialist International), most radicals were all too ready to find excuses to support "their" governments in 1914.

Many of these same individuals soon realized their mistake as the war dragged on. Moreover, it is important to remember that the urge of nationalism which greeted the outbreak of war was far from universal. Yet nationalism is basically a matter of emotion. Few revolutionaries found a way to reconcile internationalist beliefs with the patriotic passions of many of the common people.

Underlying all of these problems was the determinism which infected most revolutionaries. Like many people born in the nineteenth century, there existed on the left an almost childlike faith in human progress. Put simply, the European left thought society would, almost automatically, get better. The revolutionaries' job was to speed up the process, but somehow, few thought their opponents could stop this historically ordained march to a more just society. This perennial optimism led to a type of determinism which repeatedly paralyzed Europe's revolutionaries in times of crisis. Further, the members of the left could not easily conceive that either the bourgeoisie or the governments of Europe would turn to repression of a qualitatively more drastic nature. That is, in times of reaction, short prison sentences were expected, and outright murder was not.

Divisions within the Left

Naturally, it would be an error to place all the blame for the revolutionary left's failures on external factors. In addition to the movement's tendency to think societal development would eliminate many difficulties (like the peasantry) the bitter splits and divisions which inevitably plagued the left must be added. This should come as no surprise given the wide variety of different tactics, strategies and even goals promoted by people who may be considered members of the revolutionary camp. In fact, it is in many ways more remarkable that so much unity existed among the members of the left.

Of the almost countless schisms and strife, only a few major splits need be repeated here. Within the First International, the dispute between socialists and anarchists helped rip the organization apart. Later the Socialist movements were torn between reformists, who believed in a peaceful road to socialism, and revolutionaries, who believed that the existing state structure had to be smashed. The First World War and the Russian Revolution which followed resulted in the heightening of existing differences. As a result, some formed new Communist parties and some remained with the established Socialists parties.

Outside their historical context, these disputes often appear pointless or even petty. However, real differences existed which could not be wished away. Ultimately anarchists, with their belief in individual terror, could not be expected to cooperate with socialists, intent on organizing mass, collective actions. It was probably not only inevitable, but even healthy that these splits occurred. What was sometimes counterproductive was the amount of effort and time which was wasted in the struggle between the competing tendencies. In attempts to woo potential supporters and highlight differences with rivals, various radical tendencies frequently lost their focus. Common interests and common enemies were all too often forgotten in the heat of organizational contention. Still, looked at dispassionately, it can be argued that amount of solidarity which existed was indeed great.

Finally, it must be noted that the revolutionary left failed in part because it was victim of its own successes. Although it never achieved its ultimate goals, the left did make any number of important changes in European society. These reforms, whether granted by governments out of fear or achieved through legal struggle, tended to dull the immediacy of the need for a complete revolutionary transformation. Although the list of reforms is too lengthy to give here, their range is impressive ranging from the abolition of child labor and compulsory free education to universal adult suffrage. Of course, none of these were achieved without non-radical allies but few could have been achieved without the left. Once the Bolsheviks came to power in Russia, every blunder or injustice ascribed to their regime would be nailed to the body of those who believed in revolution.

Legacy of the European Revolutionary Left

Given all their failures and mistakes, it would be reasonable to ask what significance these movements, ideas, and individuals can hold for future generations. After all, did the left fail in its goal of establishing a classless society? What, if anything, can be said of its legacy? To appreciate this legacy, it must be remembered that the revolutionary left helped change the world even when falling short of its ultimate goals.

Firstly, these European rebels raised questions which others had previously not even considered. The importance of social class, while not invented by the left, was crucial to promoting an alternative world view to the nationalism which was surging throughout European society. The idea that workers shared common interests and should unite in common struggle was a powerful notion which helped raise the hitherto inarticulate masses onto the stage of human history. By advancing the question of class, repeatedly and with determination, the revolutionary left helped popularize the belief that legal equality meant little for those in dire economic circumstances. As the satirist, Anatole France (1844–1924), wryly commented it is "the majesty of the law which forbids both poor and rich alike from begging on the public streets or sleeping under bridges."

Further, the left's focus on class was part of its attempt, at least partially successful, to expand the definition of freedom. That is, the left wanted freedom to go beyond formal, legal freedoms and encompass the right to eat, work, and enjoy life. For revolutionaries, liberty meant little if it was only enshrined in legal codes within an unequal and exploitative society. This is not to suggest that political freedoms were unimportant or trivial for most of the revolutionary left. On the contrary, Europe's radicals, in their great majority, struggled for generations to expand the right to vote until it included all adults regardless of class, race, or gender.

Further, it was the left which wished to expand democracy by abolishing old feudal relics based on birth such as monarchies or the British House of Lords. As regards civil liberties, revolutionaries helped fight against the intrusion of government into the personal affairs of individuals whether concerning sexuality or religion. The only "freedom" which revolutionaries rejected was the freedom to exploit or oppress other humans. These political and moral values remain shared by millions today, most of whom would not consider themselves left-wing, let alone revolutionary. Of course, this set of moral values is by no means unique to the revolutionary left. Still, if there had been no radical struggles, would these values be so widely accepted?

Another major feat which needs to be added to the balance sheet of the left is the fierce challenge mounted to the long standing belief in human inequality. Throughout the nineteenth century and into the twentieth, the inequality of human beings was widely accepted as if a natural law. This belief in "supermen" or superior races and "subhumans" or inferior races was not a view limited only to fascists or the extreme right. Even among those who might be considered well meaning, or in more recent terms, liberal, inequality was a given. If someone was poor, it was, after all, their fault. Besides, the manual laborer and the peasant were, of course, stupid. They could be given charity, but much of society never considered the prospect of educating the lower classes. Despite all their hesitations and failings of their own, the members of the left countered with the argument that all people were capable of being educated and should be treated with dignity. For the leftists, the existence of lower classes did not prove a "natural order" but, rather, reinforced the inequality of the social structure, for they viewed such classes as products of society. While this debate is far from over, the fact remains that the reasoning put forth by the left was a powerful counter to the acceptance of inequality as a "natural" order.

Likewise the "woman question" was promoted at a time when few other men showed much interest, let alone sympathy, for the victims of sexism. While it is true that many members of the left were far from free of chauvinism, nonetheless, it was Europe's radicals who most consistently fought for women's rights. The now widely accepted idea of "equal pay for equal work" was first raised by radicals who refused to embrace the prevailing notion that there existed a natural inequality between the sexes. Moreover, it was within revolutionary organizations that women were first allowed access to leadership positions. In fact, it is unthinkable that a Rosa Luxemburg could have led a movement on the right. Naturally, arguing for the abolition of discrimination based on sexual preference was seen, by conservatives, as further proof that the left was beyond the pale of polite society.

Nor should we the left be with achievements limited only to the plane of theory or morality. The radical women and men, who fought for what they saw as "a better world in birth," deserve to be remembered as part of the historical struggles which achieved very real, concrete gains for average Europeans. By fighting for a better, less oppressive world, revolutionaries forced the capitalists to grant important concessions to workers: shorter hours, higher pay, social security, expanded public education, workman's compensation, and so on. While the threat of social revolution was certainly not the only factor which led to these changes, it was certainly a pivotal part of the historical process. Nor did these struggles take place solely in the past, as witness the victory of the Socialist-Communist-Green coalition in the 1997 French parliamentary elections.

Specifically, examine the issue of leisure time for industrial workers. In the late nineteenth century, French socialist Paul Lafargue (1842–1911), Marx's son-in-law, wrote the *Right to be Lazy* which was one of the first works to argue that relaxation was a basic human right. A century later, many West European industrial workers enjoyed vacation rights which made them the envy of the world. By 1993, members of the industrial proletariat could expect to enjoy yearly vacations averaging over five weeks in Finland, thirty-two days in Italy, over four weeks in West Germany. Swedish workers receive thirty days off a year, twenty-seven days in France, twenty-five days in Great Britain and Denmark, only half a day less than those two in Spain, twenty-four days in Switzerland, Portugal offers twenty-two days holiday while Norway gives twenty-one. Meanwhile, outside Europe workers fare far less well. Even in two of the wealthiest economies, those of the United States and Japan, workers receive only a fraction of the vacation enjoyed by the average European. In the USA, an industrial worker averages only twelve days a year while in Japan workers receive a miserly eleven. What is true for vacation time also holds for other aspects of workers overall living conditions such as medical care, education, retirement benefits, job security, and child care. Of course, this is a big leap and can be disputed, yet nations where the left was strongest tend to have the highest standard and quality of life on the planet.

By curbing the worse excesses of an impersonal market system, the revolutionary left helped make the world a kinder place. Still, as Marx noted, "the rich will do everything for the poor except to get off their backs." That is to say, many of the left's most important and fundamental goals remain unfulfilled. These remain a challenge to those of later generations who share the vision of world free from exploitation, oppression, war, and prejudice. If the people who served as the subject of this book could address but a few words to the future from their graves, they might be content to remind their audience of the words of the African-American author, Frederick Douglass (1817–1895), who wrote: "If there is no struggle, there is no progress."

For Further Reading

The amount of material available on the European revolutionary left is massive even if one limits themselves to English language sources. No effort was made to include the immense body of philosophical texts which treat various aspects of revolutionary theory. Therefore, this bibliographical essay will necessarily be incomplete. Those interested in the theoretical aspects of the left would be well served by Tom Bottomore, ed., *A Dictionary of Marxist Thought* (Oxford, 1991) which also contains an excellent bibliography. To explore further the impact of women within the European left, there is the excellent reference work compiled by Sheila Rowbotham, *Women's Liberation and Revolution: A Bibliography* (London, 1972). What follows then is a representative selection of some of the most influential, significant and readily available works on the European left. For the most current research, readers are well advised to consult the numerous historical journals which cover this topic. Among the most focused and useful of these are *International Labor and Working Class History*, *Left History*, *Socialist History*, *History Workshop* and *Revolutionary History*.

There exist a number of general surveys of European socialism, labor and radicalism. Among the most useful are David Caute, *The Left in Europe since 1789* (New York, 1971), which is richly illustrated and, thus, gives the eye as well as the mind a feel for the subject. In addition, Albert S. Lindemann, *A History of European Socialism* (New Haven, 1983), which gives more depth to the theoretical problems confronting the left as well as Wolfgang Abendroth, *A Short History of the European Working Class* (London, 1972), which expertly and concisely introduces the new comer to the broad outlines of European labor particularly it's revolutionary wing. Another quite well done general study is Leslie Derfler, *Socialism Since Marx: A Century of the European Left* (New York, 1973) while the issue of internationalism is deftly addressed by the essays in Frits van Holthoon & Marcel van der Linden, eds., *Internationalism in the Labour Movement, 1830–1940* (Leiden, 1988). For those who wish to follow the left beyond the scope of this work, they would be well advised to consult Donald Sasson, *One Hundred Years of Socialism* (New York, 1997), which is particularly strong on the last half of the twentieth century.

To understand the impact of the early industrial revolution on the common people of Great Britain, one can not ask for a more insightful work than E.P. Thompson's classic *The Making of the English Working Class* (New York, 1966). A contemporary account which gives valuable witness to the condition of English workers is Henry Mayhew, *London Labour and the London Poor*, 4 vols. (London, 1861–62) as is the engaged radical critique of

Frederick Engels in his *The Condition of the Working Class in England* (London, 1987). The main personalities of the Chartist movement, which was largely a response to the problems of this time, are introduced by G.D.H. Cole in *Chartist Portraits* (London, 1941).

European Radicalism in 1871

The International Working Men's Association is detailed in a number of documentary histories that have large selections of material from their most significant deliberations. Among the most useful are *Founding of the First International: A Documentary Record* (New York, 1937), Institute of Marxism-Leninism, *Documents of the First International*, 5 vols (London, 1962–1964) and Institute of Marxism-Leninism, *Hague Congress of the First International*, 2 vols (Moscow, 1976–1978). For a selection of the writings of Marx on the IWMA, see Saul K. Padover, ed., *Karl Marx on the First International*, (New York, 1973). For a more general introduction into Marx's thought, consult the very useful Ernst Fischer, *How to Read Karl Marx*, (New York, 1996).

The Paris Commune has been well covered by historians with two of the best studies being Frank Jellinek, *The Paris Commune of 1871* (New York, 1965) and Steward Edwards, *The Paris Commune, 1871* (London, 1971). Edwards also has produced a slimmer volume with wonderful illustrations and documents entitled *The Commundards of Paris, 1871* (London, 1973). For an account of the Commune written by an important participant, consult Prosper Lissagaray, *History of the Commune* (London, 1886) while Karl Marx and Frederick Engels, *On the Paris Commune* (Moscow, 1971) brings together the classic Marxist writings on the events of 1871. Often overlooked, but invaluable, is Edith Thomas, *The Women Incendiaries* (New York, 1966), which corrects the omission of women in so many treatments of the Commune.

For an admirable treatment of the early years of what was to be the most important force within 19th-century socialism, consult Richard W. Reichard, *Crippled from Birth: German Social Democracy, 1844–1870* (Ames, Iowa, 1969). Margot Finn in *After Chartism: Class and Nation in English Radical Politics, 1848–1884* (Cambridge, 1993) sketches the English radicalism from the decline of Chartism in the late 1840s to the rise of socialist parties in the 1880s. A more general survey which discusses the conflict between Marxist and anarchist ideologies is contained in G.D.H. Cole, *Socialist Thought: Marxism and Anarchism, 1850–1890* (London, 1961) while David McLellan in his *Marx Before Marxism* (London, 1970) gives a concise portrait of the most important revolutionary of this period.

Birth and Development of European Left Radicalism

A good solid introduction to the development of trade unionism is contained in Jürgen Kuczynski, *The Rise of the Working Class* (New York, 1967). A comparative approach reveals interesting contrasts as well as similarities between two of the most important trade union movements in Wolfgang J. Mommsen and Hans-Gerhard Husung, eds., *The Development of Trade Unionism in Great Britain and Germany, 1880–1914,* (London, 1985) while Eric Hobsbawm's *Workers* (New York, 1984) is recommended for anyone who wishes to study this topic in more depth. German labor is the focus of the superb by Richard W. Reichard, *From Petition to the Strike: A History of Strikes in Germany, 1869–1914* (New York, 1991).

The growth of European socialist parties is outlined with great skill in Gary P. Steenson, *After Marx, Before Lenin: Marxism and Social-ist Working-Class Parties in Europe, 1884–1914* (Pittsburgh, 1991) while the largest party is given exquisite treatment in Raymond H. Dominick, III, *Wilhelm Liebknecht and the Foundation of the German Social Democratic Party*, (Chapel Hill, N.C., 1982) and Vernon L. Lidtke, *The Outlawed Party: Social Democracy in Germany, 1878–1890*, (Prince-ton, 1966). A study of one of the most notable leaders of the German movement is contained in William A. Pelz, *Wilhelm Liebknecht and German Social Democracy: A Documentary History* (Westport, CT, 1994) while Frank Mecklenburg and Manfred Stassen have edited a collec-tion of *German Essays on Socialism in the Nineteenth Century* (New York, 1990), which allow the English-speaking reader a representative selections of German socialist writings. Additional valuable informa-tion and insight is to be found in Dick Geary, *Aspects of German Labour, 1871–1933*, (New York, 1992) and the local study by Molly Nolan entitled *Social Democracy and Society, Working-Class Radicalism in Düsseldorf, 1890–1920* (Cambridge, 1981).For more on the interplay between workers of different ethnic backgrounds, see: John J.Kulczycki, *The Foreign Worker and the German Labor movement: Xenophobia and Solidarity in the Coal Fields of the Ruhr, 1871–1914* (Oxford, 1994). A useful comparison of a socialist movement in a smaller nation is Klaus Misgeld, et al., eds., *Creating Social Democracy: A Century of the Social Democratic Labor Party in Sweden* (University Park, Pa., 1992). For a glance at Russian radical politics in this period, one may refer to Samuel H. Baron, *Plekhanov: The Father of Russian Marxism* (London, 1963).

For a invaluable discussion of the role of women in 19th-century radical movements, the comparative approach of Sheila Rowbotham in *Women In Movement: Feminism and Social Action* (New York, 1992) is without match while her *Women, Resistance and Revolution* (London, 1972) is likewise of great worth. In addition, the former updates her earlier bibliography on women's liberation and revolution. The classic socialist approach to this question is most clearly detailed in Freder-ick Engels, *The Origin of the Family, Private Property and the State* (New York, 1972), August Bebel, *Woman Under Socialism* (New York, 1971) and in Eleanor Marx-Aveling and Edward Aveling, *The Woman Question* (London, 1886).

The classic introductory study of the Socialist International remains James Joll's *The Second International, 1889–1914* (New York, 1966) while Julius Braunthal, *History of the International*, Vol I: 1864–1914 (New York, 1967) is also of great merit. Another work which remains well worth consulting is G.D.H. Cole, *The Second International, 1889–1914* (London, 1956).

To study the major left-wing challenge to socialism, there exist a number of good introductions like George Woodcock, *Anarchism* (London, 1963), Daniel Guérin, *Anarchism* (New York, 1970) and James Joll, *The Anarchists* (London, 1964). A good case study which remains many of the nuances of this movement is contained in George R. Esenwein, *Anarchist Ideology and the Working-Class Movement in Spain, 1868–1898* (Berkeley, 1989).

Two classic texts promoting the anarchist world view are Michael Bakunin, *God and the State* (New York, 1883) and Prince Peter Kropotkin, *Selected Writings on Anarchism and Revolution* (Cambridge, MA., 1970).

To gain insight into the syndicalist movement, one would be well served by F.F. Ridley, *Revolutionary Syndicalism in France* (Cambridge, 1970), Arthur D. Lewis, *Syndicalism and the General Strike* (London, 1912) and B. Holton, *British Syndicalism, 1900–1914* (London, 1976). An important theoretical work which influenced this and other movements is Georges Sorel, *Reflections on Violence* (Glencoe, Ill., 1950).

Splits within the European Left Before World War I

The controversy between reformists and revisionists is skillfully introduced by the classic work of Peter Gay in his *The Dilemma of Democratic Socialism, Eduard Bernstein's Challenge to Marx* (New York, 1952). To read some of the original arguments, consult Eduard Bernstein, *Evolutionary Socialism* (New York, 1912) which began the debate as well as the response by Rosa Luxemburg in *Reform or Revolution?* (New York, 1970). For a restatement of the then orthodox socialist position, see Karl Kautsky, *The Social Revolution* (London,

1909) while V.I. Lenin's writings in *Selected Works,* 3 vols. (Moscow, 1970) will give the Bolshevik point of view.

The thoughts and feelings of the average European are often lost amidst philosophical discussions of theoreticians. A useful correction to this tendency is found in titles which allow the common people to speak for themselves. Among worthwhile contributions are Mark Traugott, ed., *The French Worker: Autobiographies from the Early Industrial Era* (Berkeley, 1993) as well as Alfred Kelly's *The German Worker: Working-Class Autobiographies from the Age of Industrialization,* (Berkeley, 1987) and most recently Mary Jo Maynes, *Taking the Hard Road: Life Course in French and German Workers' Autobiographies in the Era of Industrialization* (Chapel Hill and London, 1995.) The stories of individuals who became attracted to British socialism is well told in *How I Became a Socialist: A Series of Biographical Sketches* (London, 1978), while Richard J. Evans, *Proletarians and Politics: Socialism, Protest and the Working Class in Germany before the First World War,* (New York, 1990) applies scholarly analysis to working class articulation. A female perspective is available in Adelheid Popp, *The Autobiography of a Working Woman* (Chicago, 1913). To more fully appreciate how distinct working class life was from others in society, one should read the insightful work of Vernon Lidtke in *The Alternative Culture: Socialist Labor in Imperial Germany* (New York, 1985).

Left Confronts Militarism, Colonialism and Rebellion

In order to gain a general appreciation of the period of colonial expansion, there exists Eric Hobsbawm's *The Age of Empire, 1875–1914* (New York, 1987) while the specific response of workers to the Boer War is skillfully discussed in Richard Price, *An Imperial War and the British Working Class* (London, 1972). Another useful work on this conflict is Stephen Koss, ed., *The Pro-Boers: The Anatomy of an Antiwar Movement* (Chicago, 1973). To place the dilemma of the left as concerns empire in a theoretical context, one would be well served by Anthony Brewer's *Marxist Theories of Imperialism: A Critical Survey* (London, 1995).

To understand the centrality which revolutionaries gave to the threat of war, consult the detailed account by S.F. Kissin in *War and the Marxists: Socialist Theory and Practice in Capitalist Wars* (London, 1988), which includes much valuable material on lesser known conflicts like the Balkan wars. A well done case study of the response of the Socialist International to one specific crisis is contained in J. Jemnitz, *The Danger of War and the Second International (1911)*, (Budapest, 1972). The conflicts over this and other issues in Europe's largest workers party is analyzed in the classic work of Carl E. Schorske: *German Social Democracy, 1905–1917: The Development of the Great Schism* (New York, 1955). Meanwhile, a valuable biography of one of the leading French anti-war radicals is Harvey Goldberg, *Jean Jaurès* (Madison, 1962).

The aborted revolution of 1905 in Russia has been studied in depth. Among the useful introductions is Sidney Harcave, *The Russian Revolution of 1905* (London, 1970). For a brilliant, if obviously less than disinterested, account by one of 1905's key participants, see Leon Trotsky, *1905* (Harmondsworth, 1973). The orthodox Bolshevik interpretation can be found in V.I. Lenin's *Lecture on the 1905 Revolution* (Moscow, 1968).

From War to Revolution, Europe 1914–1917

The collapse of the left in face of World War I is a problem which has attracted many scholars. Among the most useful treatments in English are: Merle Fainsod, *International Socialism and the World War* (Cambridge, MA., 1935) and the wonderful work of Georges Haupt, *Socialism and the Great War: The Collapse of the Second International* (Oxford, 1973) as well as the sections in Julius Braunthal's *History of the International*, Vol II: 1914–1945 (New York, 1967), which deal with this crisis.

The effect of the war on the common people of Europe is nicely introduced by John Williams in *The Other Battlefield: The Home Fronts: Britain, France and Germany* (Chicago, 1972). Two serviceable studies of individual nations are Patrick Fridenson, ed., *The French Home Front, 1914–1918* (Oxford, 1992) and the time-honored work of Gerald D.

Feldman, *Army, Industry and Labor in Germany, 1914–1918* (Princeton, N.J., 1966). For an interesting British Labour Party view of their counterparts in Germany during the war see: Edwyn Bevan, *German Social Democracy During the War* (London, 1918).

Any serious study of the Russian Revolutions of 1917 would profit by consulting Harold Shukman, ed., *The Blackwell Encyclopedia of the Russian Revolution* (Oxford, 1988) while Paul LeBlanc provides an insightful interpretation of *Lenin and the Revolutionary Party* (Atlantic Highlands, 1990). A number of Americans have written on their impressions of Revolutionary Russia. Among the many which are openly sympathetic are John Reed, *Ten Days that Shook the World* (New York, 1934) and Louise Bryant, *Six Red Months in Russia* (London, 1982). A useful addition to these is the early part of Armand Hammer, *Hammer* (New York, 1987) which gives the viewpoint of an open minded but committed U.S. capitalist. No investigation of the events of 1917 is truly complete without Leon Trotsky, *History of the Russian Revolution* (New York, 1980), which may be supplemented by his *My Life* (New York, 1970). To understand the role of women in these dramatic events, one could not ask for a better introduction than Barbara Evans Clements, *Daughters of Revolution: A History of Women in the U.S.S.R.* (Arlington Heights, Ill., 1994).

Revolutionary Europe, 1917–1921

An unusually fine collection of essays which will help introduce the major contours of this period is contained in Chris Wrigley, ed., *Challenges of Labour: Central and Western Europe, 1917–1920* (London, 1993). To consult the proclamations issued by revolutionaries, consult the well edited collection of Helmut Gruber, *International Communism in the Era of Lenin* (Garden City, 1972). An insightful Marxist analysis of the reasons behind the failure of European revolution is contained in C.L.R. James, *World Revolution, 1917–1936: The Rise and Fall of the Communist International* (Atlantic Highlands, N.J., 1993) while another scholar from this viewpoint raises interesting questions in Donny Gluckstein, *The Western Soviets: Workers Councils versus Parliament*

1915–1920 (London, 1985). Not surprisingly, the veteran historian of European labor, Eric Hobsbawm, makes numerous thought-provoking points in his *Revolutionaries* (London, 1973).

The pivotal struggle in Germany is presented with skill by Sebastian Haffner, *Failure of a Revolution: Germany 1918/19* (London, 1973) while William A. Pelz, *The Spartakusbund and the German Working Class Movement, 1914–1919* (Lewiston, N.Y., 1988) gives additional detail. In addition, Chris Harman, *The Lost Revolution, Germany 1918–1923* (London, 1982) is of interest. To gain an understand for the most essential personality on the German revolutionary left, J.P. Nettl, *Rosa Luxemburg* (New York, 1966) is without peer while Mary-Alice Waters, ed., *Rosa Luxemburg Speaks* (New York, 1970) collects the most well known of her works. An interesting biography of the leader of the Bavarian Soviet Republic has been written by his widow, see Rosa Leviné-Meyer, *Leviné: the Life of a Revolutionary* (London, 1973).

A concise but invaluable selection of writings from the Austrian left is presented by Tom Bottomore & Patrick Goode, eds., *Austro-Marxism* (Oxford, 1978). To grapple with the complex of anti-Semitism, one will discover a wonderfully nuanced and sophisticated study in Bruce F. Pauley, *From Prejudice to Persecution: A History of Austrian Anti-Semitism* (Chapel Hill, 1992), which suggests interpretations which may go beyond just Austria. To gain an insight into the mind set of the Italian revolutionary left, consult the writings by its most renowned member Antonio Gramsci, *Gramsci: Pre-Prison Writings*, (Cambridge, 1994).

For an introduction to the social crisis which hit Great Britain during and after the First World War, see the excellent volume Walter Kendall, *The Revolutionary Movements in Britain 1900–21* (London, 1969) while a more concise title worth consulting is Chanie Rosenberg, *Britain on the Brink of Revolution, 1919* (London, 1987). The unrest within the British military is chronicled in Andrew Rothstein, *The Soldiers Strikes of 1919* (London, 1980) as well as Gloden Dallas & Douglas Gill, *The Unknown Army: Mutinies in the British Army in World War I* (London, 1985) while William Allison and John Fairley have written an entertaining and well documented account of one of the leading army dissidents in their *The Monocled Mutineer* (London, 1979). The theoretical underpinnings of Irish socialism are well explained in James Connolly's classic *Labour in Irish History,* (New York, 1910) while P. Berresford Ellis in *A History of the Irish Working Class,* (London, 1972) gives a good overview. For the role of the left in Ireland and particularly the Easter Rebellion, consult C. Desmond Greaves, *The Life and Times of James Connolly* (New York, 1971).

Index

Adler, Friedrich, 103–4, 119

Adler, Viktor, 29, 88–9, 103–4

Altgeld, John Peter, 31

Anarchism, 8–9, 36–9, 54–6, 66

Anti-Semitism, 50, 65, 78, 81, 119, 124–5, 137; see also Dreyfus, Alfred

Anti-socialist law, 42–4, 46

Austro-Marxism, 119–21

Bakunin, Mikhail, 39, 83

Bauer, Otto, 119, 120, 124

Bax, Belfort, 97

Bebel, August, 23, 24–5, 29, 34, 49, 62, 65, 84, 91, 92, 103, 124

Bernstein, Eduard, 47–50, 54, 61–3, 71

Biennio Rosso, 126–8

Bismarck, Otto von, 11–2, 14, 17, 38, 43, 52

Boer War, 71, 73–6; see also Colonialism

Bolsheviks, 52–4, 82–3, 98–9, 100–1, 104–10, 114

Bonaparte, Louis, 11

Bonaparte, Napoleon, 11, 85

Briand, Aristide, 58

Chartists, 26

Clemenceau, Georges, 58

Colonialism, 61, 65, 70–77, 134, 139–40; see also Boer War, Racism

Communist parties
    Austria, 121
    Germany, 48, 68, 103, 116–8
    Hungary, 122
    Russia, see Bolsheviks

Connolly, James, 131–2

Doyle, Arthur Conan, 74

Dreyfus, Alfred, 50

Ebert, Friedrich, 115–6, 120

Eisner, Kurt, 117–8

Engels, Frederick, 3–4, 9, 16, 34, 47, 62, 92, 124, 137

Fascism, 4, 42, 43, 116, 127, 128, 134, 135, 143; see also Freikorps

France, Anatole, 143

Franco, Francisco, 28

Franco-Prussian War, 8, 10–1, 16, 29, 85, 91

Freikorps, 117–9

Gallifet, Gaston, 50–1

Gars, Jean, 51

George, David Loyd, 95

Grimm, Robert, 100

Guesde, Jules, 26, 51

Haase, Hugo, 89, 103

Hardie, Keir, 26, 89

Hitler, Adolf, 28, 115, 116, 120, 124, 129; see also Fascism; Anti-Semitism

Iglesias, Pablo, 26

Imperialism

Internationals
    First (IWMA), 5–10, 24, 30, 71
    Second, 29–34, 36, 39, 47, 51–2, 59–60, 63, 66–9, 76–7, 88–9, 101, 139
    Third, 33, 72, 121

Jaurès, Jean, 51, 68, 88, 89, 92

Kamenev, Lev, 108

Karl I, 119

Kautsky, Karl, 28, 47–9, 53, 54, 69, 76, 88, 115

Kerensky, Alexander, 106, 107, 109, 115

Kropotkin, Peter, 69, 83, 92, 97

Kun, Béla, 122–4, 134

Labriola, Antonio, 48
Lafargue, Paul, 144
Larkin, James. 131–2
Ledebour, Georg, 103
Legien, Karl, 89
Lenin, Vladimir Ilyich, 16, 34, 48, 49,
    52–4, 83, 88, 91, 100–1, 105, 107–
    10
Leviné, Eugene, 118, 124
Liebknecht, Karl, 99, 102–3, 113, 115–7,
    134
Liebknecht, Wilhelm, 24, 29, 49, 68, 92
Lincoln, Abraham, 10, 71
Ludendorff, Erich von, 112–3, 115
Luxemburg, Rosa, 48–9, 54, 62–63, 83,
    85, 99, 112, 115, 116–7, 124, 138,
    143
Marx, Karl, 4, 7–9, 16, 37, 47, 53, 71,
    135, 138
Marxism, 7, 13, 22–6, 29, 33–4, 45
May Day, 30–4, 42, 106
Mehring, Franz, 99, 117
Mensheviks, 52–4
Merrheim, Alphonse, 102
Militarism, 65–9
Millerand, Alexandre, 50–2, 54, 57–8;
    see also Reformism
Mussolini, Benito, 28, 41, 92, 127, 128
Nationalism, 65–6, 72–3, 87–89, 92
Nicholas II, 79, 81, 104
Owen, Robert, 26
Paris Commune, 5, 8, 10–16, 17, 30,
    50–51
Pétain, Henri-Philippe, 129–30
Plekhanov, Georgy, 47–8, 67
Racism, 61, 65, 72–3; see also Anti-
    Semitism; Fascism, Colonialism
Reformism and revisionism, 45–52; see
    also Bernstein, Eduard
Religion, 4, 14, 22–3, 27, 35, 60–4, 69,
    78, 137–8; see also Anti-Semitism
Revolutions
    France, 11

Germany, 114–6
Ireland, 131–3
Hungary, 121–4
Russia, 77–82, 104–10
See also Paris Commune
Rhodes, Cecil, 73
Scheidemann, Philipp, 73, 115, 120
Serrati, Giacinto, 101, 128
Smith, Adam, 22
Social democratic and labour parties
    Austria, 26, 29–30, 89, 98, 119–21,
        125; see also Adler, Viktor;
        Austro-Marxism
    Belgium, 24, 26, 36, 98
    Denmark, 26, 84
    France, 26, 50–2
    Germany, 5, 24, 32, 38, 43–50, 72–
        3, 91, 102–3, 115; see also
        Liebknecht, Wilhelm; Bebel,
        August; Ebert, Friedrich;
        Anti-socialist laws
    Great Britain, 19–20, 23, 26, 75, 93,
        100, 102
    Ireland, 131–2
    Italy, 51, 72, 92, 98, 99, 126–8
    Netherlands, 26, 67, 98
    Norway, 26, 98
    Russia, 52–4
    Spain, 26
    Sweden, 26, 59–60, 84, 98
    Switzerland, 26, 99–100
Stalin, Joseph, 28, 54, 110, 134
Syndicalism, 19–20, 140–1, 51, 56–9, 63,
    66, 67, 72, 83–4, 89, 92, 131
Thiers, Adolphe, 12, 15
Trade unions, 17–23;
    France, 19, 40–1, 56–60, 63, 89, 98,
        130
    Germany, 19–20, 33, 43, 60, 85, 89
    Great Britain, 6, 20, 22, 29, 32–3,
        60, 102
    Ireland, 131–2
    Spain, 56–7

United States, 19, 131
Trotsky, Leon, 28, 80, 83, 107, 112, 124, 137
Turati, Filippo, 51, 71
Twain, Mark, 71
Webb, Sidney, 71
Wilhelm I, 38, 43
Wilhelm II, 50, 102, 114
Wilson, Woodrow, 87, 111
Women's emancipation, 13–4, 34–6, 95–6, 121, 138–9
World War I, 91–9, 111–4
Zetkin, Clara, 29, 34, 49, 99, 116–7
Zimmerwald Conference, 99–101, 106
Zinoviev, Grigori, 108

Studies in Modern European History

The monographs in this series focus upon aspects of the political, social, economic, cultural, and religious history of Europe from the Renaissance to the present. Emphasis is placed on the states of Western Europe, especially Great Britain, France, Italy, and Germany. While some of the volumes treat internal developments, others deal with movements such as liberalism, socialism, and industrialization, which transcend a particular country.

The series editor is:

Frank J. Coppa
Director, Doctor of Arts Program
in Modern World History
Department of History
St. John's University
Jamaica, New York 11439

To order other books in this series, please contact our Customer Service Department:

(800) 770-LANG (within the U.S.)
(212) 647-7706 (outside the U.S.)
(212) 647-7707 FAX

or browse online by series at:
WWW.PETERLANG.COM